A Court of Refuge

A Court of Refuge

STORIES FROM THE BENCH OF AMERICA'S FIRST MENTAL HEALTH COURT

Judge Ginger Lerner-Wren
with Rebecca A. Eckland

BEACON PRESS
BOSTON

BEACON PRESS
Boston, Massachusetts
www.beacon.org

Beacon Press books
are published under the auspices of
the Unitarian Universalist Association of Congregations.

21 20 19 18   8 7 6 5 4 3 2 1

This book is printed on acid-free paper that meets the uncoated paper
ANSI/NISO specifications for permanence as revised in 1992.

Text design and composition by Kim Arney

Many names and identifying characteristics of people mentioned
in this work have been changed to protect their identities.

Library of Congress Cataloging-in-Publication Data

Names: Lerner-Wren, Ginger, author. | Eckland, Rebecca A., author.
Title: A court of refuge : stories from the bench of America's first mental
health court / Ginger Lerner-Wren, Rebecca A. Eckland.
Description: Boston, Massachusetts : Beacon Press, 2018. | Includes
bibliographical references and index.
Identifiers: LCCN 2017044843 (print) | LCCN 2017045126 (ebook) |
ISBN 9780807086995 (ebook) | ISBN 9780807086988 (hardback)
Subjects: LCSH: Mental health courts—United States. | Mentally ill
offenders—Legal status, laws, etc.—United States. | People with mental
disabilities and crime—United States. | Criminal justice, Administration of—
United States. | BISAC: LAW / Disability. | MEDICAL / Mental Health. |
BIOGRAPHY & AUTOBIOGRAPHY / Lawyers & Judges.
Classification: LCC KF3828.5 (ebook) | LCC KF3828.5 .L47 2018 (print) |
DDC 345.73/01—dc23
LC record available at https://lccn.loc.gov/2017044843

To Aaron and the Wynn family

CONTENTS

AUTHOR'S NOTE

In 1996 I was elected a judge of the county court of Broward County, Florida, the Seventeenth Judicial Circuit, and my term formally began in January 1997. Chief Judge Dale Ross (now retired) assigned me to the Criminal Division. On June 6, 1997, he signed the administrative order that established America's first mental health court.[1] This order recognized the essential need for a new system of justice to focus on individuals with mental health disabilities, arrested for misdemeanor offenses and the need for appropriate treatment in a therapeutic environment conducive to wellness (not punishment) as well as continuing to ensure the protection of the public.

Further, to help defendants who desire such treatment, the order recognized the need for a judge with expertise in the field of mental health and therefore possessed the needed understanding and ability to expeditiously and efficiently move people from jail into community mental health care, without compromising the safety of the public.

For the first time in the United States, a specialized problem-solving court was dedicated to the decriminalization of people with mental health problems and to use the court process to link individuals with community-based mental health care, from a recovery-oriented perspective.

Per the order, the court is part-time; technically it is a subdivision of my Criminal Division, so I preside over both a traditional criminal division and the mental health court. The administrative order provided that the court would be voluntary. Its jurisdiction would include all misdemeanor offenses, except driving under the influence and domestic violence offenses. The order also denoted that "battery cases could be accepted, with victim's consent." Defendants who may access the court included those with psychiatric diagnoses included in the *Diagnostic and Statistical Manual of Mental Disorders*, fourth edition (commonly known as the *DSM-IV*) as well as neurological and cognitive disorders such as traumatic brain injuries, dementia, intellectual disabilities, and learning disabilities.[2] The court's ability to respond rapidly to an individual's clinical treatment needs required that the court referral process be open and consumer-friendly. Anyone could refer a case to the court, and the docketing was spontaneous to allow cases to be heard in court without delay.

The mental health court is dedicated to decriminalizing those who suffer from various psychiatric conditions and diverting them from the criminal justice system into a context appropriate to their challenges. The administrative order granted me authority over the planning, design, and operational components of the court. Much of the court's design, values, philosophy, and diversionary structure is based upon my prior training in my position with the Advocacy Center for Persons with Disabilities (now Disability Rights Florida), in a dual role as PAIMI attorney (under the Protection and Advocacy of Individuals with Mental Illness Act of 1986) and plaintiff's monitor in the federal class-action suit related to South Florida State Hospital. This class action was filed in response to the lack of care and treatment for those confined to South Florida State Hospital. The complaint alleged that residents did not receive even minimal care and that the conditions of the hospital were physically and emotionally debilitating. The case was settled in 1993 with a focus on improvements to the hospital and individualized discharge planning for those returning to the community.

Even though I was a new judge, at the time the mental health court was established I was appointed because of the skills and experience I had acquired in this unique position. When I was elected

judge, at my investiture ceremony I was introduced by my former boss, Circuit Judge Marcia Beach. Judge Beach was the executive director of the Advocacy Center for Persons with Disabilities.
She was a fierce advocate of persons with disabilities. When Judge
Beach passed away in 2016, the tribute written by the reporter
Carol Marbin Miller eloquently expressed the judge's path-breaking
role: "The woman who changed how disabled people are treated has
died."[3] Judge Beach was an advocate of human rights in every as-
pect of her personal and professional life. She was a tireless advocate for persons with disabilities and demonstrated a passion for
human dignity, social inclusion, and leading social change. Judge
Beach believed in trial by fire—and believed in me. Consequently,
I have always looked upon my appointment to the mental health
court as a serendipitous acknowledgment of her legacy and her role
as my mentor.

Since that historic juncture in 1996, the insights and lessons
learned through the lived experiences of mental health court participants, their families, and their extended families has improved the
culture of our court system. It has helped to change minds and attitudes about mental illness and how we think about mental health
as a whole. The stories shared in this book reflect actual case histories, but names, identities, and some facts have been altered to protect confidentiality. There are, however, some exceptions: Kathryn
Steeves, who graciously agreed to be interviewed for this book, and
a few individuals who appeared in the court who have passed, including Jack Kuhn and Seth Staumbach, discussed in chapter 5. I
hope that my recounting of their experiences in the mental health
court honors their lives and their noble contributions to our community and society.

A Court of Refuge

CHAPTER 1

A Race for Justice

On Tuesday, June 24, 1997, I took the bench as the lawyers and clinical team waited anxiously for me to call the first case. I said a silent prayer and nodded to my deputy to indicate that this new, specialized division—the session held during the lunch break of my regular criminal division court—was ready to begin. We were embarking on a new journey in therapeutic justice. Howard Finkelstein, the catalyst for the creation of the Broward County Mental Health Court, had envisioned "a refuge" for people arrested because of actions they had taken while suffering from mental illness and cognitive disorders. In order to create that "refuge," I needed my opening remarks to be welcoming, thoughtful, and compassionate. As I called the first case, I never imagined that in fact a new system of justice was beginning. In truth, no one could predict what a mental health court would mean or what it could do. The first defendant, Roger, was in his early twenties and homeless. As the deputies led Roger into the courtroom, I realized that he was not coherent. He had been arrested for causing a disturbance in front of a convenience store. His hair hung in long, unwashed tangles, obscuring his face from view.

As the deputies led him to a high-back leather chair in the jury box where they seated defendants who were in custody, he released the kind of scream that indicates deep emotional pain. The deputy handcuffed him to the chair, which was attached to the floor. He began to shake, and his unintelligible sounds became louder. As seconds turned to minutes, his noises turned to screams. I tried to speak to him, but it was clear he had surpassed his ability to listen.

All I could do was watch him.

His screams continued, hollow and desperate, as though this was the only form of expression he had left. As he became more agitated, he pulled on the chair, trying to free himself from the handcuffs and the chair. I had no idea if a person could exert enough force to dislodge a chair that was attached to the courtroom floor.

It was clear that there was nothing I could do from the bench for Roger, and in the interest of calming the situation, I stopped the hearing. I ordered the court staff to clear the courtroom, and since the courtroom had one door, we left the same way that Roger had entered, through the front door. Most courtrooms have two entrances, one for the judge and another for in-custody defendants, so this circumstance was unique to this courtroom. Yet the one door served as a reminder of the humanistic impulse that had led to the court's founding and my responsibility to ensure that human dignity, as well as justice, was served here today and every day the court would convene.

In the hallway, the court team huddled in a circle: Assistant State Attorneys Lee Cohen and Melissa Steinberg; Assistant Public Defender Doug Brawley; the mental health court monitor, Bertha Smith; and the mental health court clinician, Greg Forster. They waited in silence for me to do or say something. Keeping in mind the function of the court, I signed the first mental health court order for diversion in the hallway outside the courtroom. The diversion order mandated that Roger would be transferred out of jail, where he had been kept for several weeks; the emergency transportation order directed the Broward County Sheriff's Office to take Roger from the jail to the nearest psychiatric receiving facility or hospital. The order required performing an independent psychiatric screening and assessment and provision of treatment under Florida's involuntary civil commitment law (the Baker Act) if Roger met the legal criteria.[1]

Diversion orders are common to problem-solving courts. At the time that Broward began its mental health court, problem-solving courts were a relatively new development in the US criminal justice system. Miami-Dade County had established the nation's first drug treatment court in 1989 which offered substance abuse treatment as an alternative to prosecution, incarceration, or other typical criminal justice sanctions.[2] According to Bruce Winick, a professor of law and the cofounder of the science of therapeutic jurisprudence (TJ), "These courts were created to address vexing social problems which were often driven by policy vacuums in our society."[3] TJ offers the promise that a court, acting as a "therapeutic agent," can respond to psychosocial problems as well as "minister to the law."[4] Judges who write diversion orders understand that there are vacuums in society that must be filled with new laws and options. According to Winick, these vacuums may include a shortage of mental health services and a lack of sense of community, results of society's ineffectiveness to address a wide range of social problems, which then "get dumped on the doorsteps of the courthouse."[5]

In problem-solving courts, which are voluntary, people can acknowledge that they do have a problem and can participate in a non-adversarial court process allowing a judge, lawyers, and social service and treatment providers to collaborate to help them with their real human problems. Whether it is an alcohol problem or untreated mental illness, problem-solving courts provide a new way for judges to help people with their psychosocial problems and other human needs.

According to the Bureau of Justice Statistics, in 2012 there were 3,052 problem-solving courts in the United States.[6] The most common types of problem-solving courts were drug courts (44 percent of these courts) and mental health courts (11 percent). There are various types of problem-solving diversionary courts in the juvenile level as well and hybrid courts, which address both mental health and substance abuse disorders. There are also driving while under the influence (DWI) courts, which, like domestic violence courts, are not diversionary but focus on accountability and public safety. The diversionary goals of the court are intended to intercept people arrested on low-level criminal offenses, offer a therapeutic approach to the criminal case, and promote access to community-based mental health care, housing, and other support services. For people who appear in need of psychiatric hospitalization, the court's diversionary order is also designed to break arrest cycles and prevent defendants from being discharged back into the criminal justice system.

In the Broward County Mental Health Court's first hearing, I directed that my office would be notified at least twenty-four hours in advance of Roger's release from the hospital. This part of the process was important because it allowed my office to coordinate with the Broward County Sheriff's Office to bring Roger back to the court for a follow-up hearing. I did not want Roger going back into the jail system. Upon his return, I wanted the opportunity for the in-court clinician to assess Roger's stability and introduce him to the mental health court's process. It would be up to him to choose whether he wanted to participate in the court, which (like all diversion courts) is voluntary. As we stood together in the hallway trying to process what we had just witnessed, Assistant Public Defender Doug Brawley, the designated mental health supervisor for county court, was eager to see the next defendant on the docket.

"You see, Judge," he said, "I knew it was important that the court begin as soon as reasonably possible."

Clearly, Doug was right.

"You have no idea what I have witnessed in other court divisions," he said. "People with serious mental illness who were experiencing psychosis or due to intellectual challenges could not manage their behavior in front of judges."

Assistant State Attorney Lee Cohen chimed in: "Doug is right, Your Honor. Judges mean well, but they are not trained in mental health. When something like this occurs, some judges perceive that the defendants are behaving inappropriately on purpose. Doug and I have spent years running from courtroom to courtroom, as judges call for supervisors to assist them."

"Some judges threaten my clients with contempt sanctions under the mistaken belief that their behavior will improve," Doug

said. "I've tried to explain that what they are witnessing is the manifestation of a mental illness; these people aren't intentionally mis-
behaving or disrespecting the court. Nonetheless, there have been
times when my clients have been placed in restraint chairs and received disciplinary reports in the jail for their behavior. I do not
want what happened to Aaron to happen to anyone else."

At the mention of Aaron's name, we all fell silent, humbled by
the sacrifice it took to bring the Broward County Mental Health
Court into existence.

It had been a high-profile case. From the expressions on the
faces around me, I knew that the Aaron Wynn situation was on
everyone's mind. I thought about what Broward County's public
defender, Howard Finkelstein, had said. As we finalized Roger's paperwork, I wondered, *Had we created a court of refuge?*

We walked back into the courtroom, shaken and silent. After
all, what had happened to Aaron could happen to any one of us.

In 1985, when Aaron Wynn was eighteen years old—just about
Roger's age—he was struck by a car and knocked off his motorcycle. At the time, Aaron was preparing to leave home and head
for college. However, his injuries from the accident were serious
enough to erase Aaron's dream of attending college: his extensive
injuries included head trauma. He endured a series of complex sur-
geries meant to make a normal life possible for him once again. Yet,
just as his parents were starting to think that there may be some
chance for a complete recovery, they realized that the brain injuries
were more severe than anyone had realized.

The young man who had loved the ocean, sports, and playing
chess had become angry and despondent. Aaron's personality had
taken a one-eighty turn; the happy-go-lucky young man was now
quiet and constantly withdrawn. It was as though the spark inside
him had been extinguished, and all that was left was a shell.

Jane and Alexander Wynn were desperate to obtain mental
health care for their son. They called every public official and mental health agency they could, but the response was always the same:

"Aaron does not qualify for services." One factor that seemed to complicate the Wynns' attempts to find care for their son was the complex nature of his condition: there were at least seven diagnoses, ranging from schizophrenia to organic brain syndrome.

As Aaron's memory and cognitive functions continued to decline, so did his parents' hopes and dreams for their son. Over time, Aaron could not control his anger or regulate his emotions. The Wynns even tried to get Aaron admitted to South Florida State Hospital, but were told there was a two-year wait list.

In 1988—three years after his accident—Aaron was arrested for allegedly assaulting a police officer when he was not able to control his anger during an encounter. Citing Florida Statute 916, the judge found Aaron mentally incompetent to stand trial and committed him to a forensic hospital for mentally ill persons in the custody of the Department of Corrections. The Florida Department of Children and Families placed Aaron in two different hospitals: South Florida Evaluation and Treatment Center in Miami-Dade and North Florida Evaluation and Treatment Center in Chattahoochee.[7] Instead of receiving rehabilitation services there, Aaron was put in solitary confinement for two and a half years and was strapped to a gurney in four- and five-point restraints.

In 1991, for reasons unknown, Aaron was released from the forensic hospital with no discharge plan or linkage to residential placement. The Wynn family was reunited, but they found themselves in the same nightmare as before, except that Aaron's condition had significantly worsened. Aaron could not remember his parents' names. He was often delusional. Doctors now diagnosed Aaron with schizophrenia and post-traumatic stress disorder due to the maltreatment he endured at the hospital. The Wynns tried to house Aaron in local boarding homes, but Aaron's aggressive behavior always led to his eviction.

The family was trapped in a nightmare.

Two years later, in 1993, as Aaron waited in the line for the cash register of a South Florida grocery store, he suffered yet another psychiatric episode. It wasn't unusual; he suffered many psychotic episodes, for he still had an untreated mental illness. This episode, however, would once again change Aaron's life and tear the Wynn family apart.

In a panic, Aaron darted out of the grocery store and collided with Pauline Johnson, an eighty-five-year-old woman. Pauline fell to the ground, hitting her head on the concrete curb with considerable force. She died of head injuries the following day.[8]

Aaron was arrested for first-degree murder.

When Howard Finkelstein, Broward County's chief assistant public defender, was assigned to represent Aaron, he said that it "changed my life in ways that I couldn't have imagined."

Howard, known as a charismatic and highly skilled defense attorney, thought he knew how the introductory meeting with Aaron's family would go. He wasn't prepared for what would transpire at the Wynns' home in Plantation. He knew how concerned the family would be, given the seriousness of the charge. Howard planned to introduce himself and spend ample time getting acquainted with Aaron's mother and father. Then, Howard would tell them about the breadth and depth of his criminal defense experience to give them confidence and shift into an explanation of his trial strategy. It was always important to Howard that a defendant's family understand and feel comfortable with him and his plan. He knew that he would need their cooperation and support to prepare an effective defense for Aaron. He would need their help securing medical records for expert witnesses and to be fully engaged in the court process.

Recalling that meeting, Howard said, "I can't believe what I was thinking. I walked into the Wynns' living room believing that I was going to tell them what I was going to do for their son. I could not have been more wrong."

After Jane Wynn opened the front door to their home, she looked Howard in the eyes and politely asked him to sit down. "I need to tell you something," Jane said. Her eyes were filled with deep sadness as she told Aaron's story.

After meeting with Aaron's family, Howard was consumed with indignation and anger. He felt that he had to do something on a systemic level to prevent further tragedy due to the failings of

Broward County's mental health system. With the aid of assistant public defender Fred Goldstein, a mental health expert, Howard wrote to the Broward County Grand Jury to request a formal investigation of the county's mental health system.

In a ten-page letter, Howard detailed the tragic story of Aaron Wynn, Pauline Johnson, and the relationship of these tragedies and his client's arrest for murder (the charge had been reduced to manslaughter) to his inability to secure mental health care and rehabilitative services. To Howard's surprise, the grand jury approved his request.

In November 1994, after an extensive eight-month review of Broward's mental health system, the grand jury released a scathing 153-page report.[9] Among its findings, the grand jury described Broward's mental health system as "deplorable and chronically underfunded."[10] The scope of the grand jury's work was broad based and included the criminal justice system. The report also identified the overrepresentation of people with mental illness cycling between jail, emergency rooms, and homeless shelters, and it called for accountability, collaboration, and the need for expanded resources to provide those who suffered from mental illnesses with continuous care.[11]

Buoyed by the findings of the grand jury, a small group of criminal justice and mental health stakeholders, headed by Broward Circuit Court Judge Mark A. Speiser, assembled an ad hoc task force to seek solutions to streamline the processing of people arrested with serious mental illness. After several years of meetings and with no consensus in sight, Judge Speiser asked Howard, "What do you want?"

"I want my own [bleeping] court," Howard said. "A court of refuge."

In that moment, and unbeknownst to me—I was campaigning for judicial office—the task force had met, and the concept for a specialized mental health court had emerged. It would ensure due process and the promotion of individual constitutional rights while balancing public safety considerations. There was no doubt that most judges were not trained to respond to the unique needs and challenges endured by people affected by mental health conditions.

Yet, there was no road map, no funding or grants—simply "the will of a community" to improve the criminal justice system's response to the criminalization of people with mental illness in Broward County.

When the court began operations, in 1997, in the Broward County courthouse on Southeast Sixth Street in Fort Lauderdale, national data on inmates with serious mental illness were essentially nonexistent. However, a report released by the Bureau of Justice Statistics in 2001 stated that (in 1997) "nearly a third of State inmates and a quarter of Federal inmates reported having some physical impairment or mental condition."[12] Within the year, however, the *New York Times* published a groundbreaking special report, "Asylum Behind Bars." Written by Fox Butterfield, the report confirmed what many individuals and families affected by mental illness already knew: US jails and prisons had become, "by default," our nation's largest state psychiatric hospitals.[13] According to Butterfield, more than one in ten of the two hundred thousand people behind bars in the United States suffered from serious mental illness, which included major depression, bipolar disorder, and schizophrenia.[14]

The deinstitutionalization trend that began in the 1960s with the availability of new psychotropic medications, a wave of federal civil rights orders on behalf of patients' rights, and a congressional study performed by the Joint Commission on Mental Illness and Health was intended to combat the negative effects of mental illness.[15] The advancements in mental health treatment and rehabilitation led to optimism and the realization by President John F. Kennedy that people with mental illness and intellectual disorders can live humanely in the community. President Kennedy pointed to the positive research of the joint commission's final report and outlined, through a series of legislative actions commonly referred to as the Community Mental Health Act of 1963, a new vision for mental health care in America. The act was intended to shift resources away from large state psychiatric institutions toward a community-based approach that would emphasize access to care and rehabilitative services. It pointed to a visionary plan to transform mental health in

America, reflecting the belief that persons with mental disabilities deserve "to live in the open warmth of the community."[16]

Tragically, the nation's loss of President Kennedy a month after he signed the Community Mental Health Act into law created a vacuum in executive branch leadership. The goals of the act—to emphasize access to community-based mental health care, prevention, and rehabilitation—fell victim to the turmoil of the 1960s. Competing priorities to finance the Vietnam War, resistance to neighborhood mental health centers, health insurance restrictions, new civil rights laws regarding civil commitment, and a lack of funding to pay for local resources all undermined the goals of the Community Mental Health Care Act of 1963.[17]

As Fox Butterfield noted in his report for the *New York Times*, "States seized the chance to slash hospital budgets and reduce hospital beds." For example, the number of beds in state hospitals went from a high of 559,000 in 1955 to 69,000 in 1995.[18] "On any given day," Butterfield wrote, "almost 200,000 people [are] behind bars. More than 1 in 10 of the total are known to suffer from schizophrenia, manic depression or major depression [. . .] the three most severe mental illnesses."[19]

In South Florida, for example, as Aaron Wynn's parents pleaded with state mental health program directors to get Aaron into the South Florida State Hospital in Pembroke Pines, local mental health activists were waging a separate battle for increased spending for state mental health hospital beds. According to the *Sun-Sentinel*, dozens of people on a waiting list for a court-ordered state hospital bed were being warehoused in a small county crisis unit, which offered no rehabilitation.[20] In 1991, Broward County mental health advocates fought again when the number of hospital beds was reduced from 1,200 to 400. According to Sandra Jacobs, who covered the medical beat for the *Broward and Palm Beach Sun-Sentinel*, "South Florida State, designated for the most severely ill people from Key West to Vero Beach, has fewer than 11 beds for every 100,000 residents."[21]

I wondered, *What if the judge who presided over Aaron Wynn's criminal case had understood the contextual nuances of the trend known as the criminalization of mental illness? Would Aaron have been offered treat-ment instead of incarceration?*

Sitting at the bench in the mental health court after issuing Roger's diversion order, I called the next case. The next defendant, Mary Stevens, was an elderly woman who appeared to be in her late sixties or early seventies. She had been arrested for trespassing at a gas station and had been in jail for approximately forty-five days. I speculated that she was homeless. I glanced through the court file, which included an order by the originally assigned judge that declared her "mentally incompetent to stand trial." There were no future court dates or other pleadings and no defense motions for her release. Mary Stevens and her case had fallen between the cracks in the system.

"Ms. Stevens," I said, "how are you doing? My name is Judge Lerner-Wren."

There was no response.

I wondered whether she had a hearing impairment. I tried again, using the court microphone. "Ms. Stevens," I said firmly, "hello . . . can you hear me?"

I asked Greg Forster, the acting in-court clinician and a highly skilled community case manager, to check on her. Greg, known for his mild manner and boundless compassion, leaned over the jury box to speak with her. We watched to see if she responded to him. As Greg tried to speak to her, I noticed that Mary's eyes were not moving.

I yelled for my deputy to call 911. Something was wrong. Already shaken by what had occurred at the prior hearing, we looked at each other in disbelief. How many people did Doug say were on the mental health unit? The individuals whom the court had already seen were in urgent need of mental health treatment or emergency medical care. Clearly, there was an urgency to see as many people as we could in the court, as quickly as possible. According to Human Rights Watch, US prisons and jails are not equipped to address the complex needs of this population.[22] What we had witnessed in just two cases clearly supported this assertion.

Minutes seemed like hours as we waited for the emergency medical team to arrive. Finally, the paramedics rushed into the courtroom carrying a gurney. Two medics unpacked the medical equipment while the others began to triage Ms. Stevens.

"How long has she been like this?" one of the medics asked.

"I have no idea," I responded. "This is how she was when she was brought to the courtroom."

I watched as the paramedics lifted her frail, unresponsive frame onto the gurney. There was really no way of knowing how long Ms. Stevens had sat unresponsive in a jail cell, nor how long the traumatic experiences and harsh conditions of living in the street had been draining away the person she had been. How can we know how long someone has suffered when they no longer have the capacity to tell us? How can I say that Aaron Wynn's suffering was limited to the two years he spent in the hospital, restrained and alone? His suffering, I believe, stretched back to the day of his motorcycle accident, and it continues to this day.

The first mental health court docket was over. It certainly was not what I had expected; and yet, there was a sense of relief and pride knowing that individuals who needed psychiatric and medical treatment were going to receive care in a therapeutic and more appropriate healthcare setting. As we went our separate ways, I couldn't help thinking that everyone involved in the new Broward County Mental Health Court had embarked on an unknown journey.

CHAPTER 2

The Shackles Come Off

"Welcome to mental health court," I said in lieu of the formal "All rise" pronouncement to the open court. The informality is important. The phrase helps to set the tone for a courtroom culture where human dignity, therapeutic justice, and the rule of law coexist. In mental health court, I have learned, small things often can make a big difference.

Within the first year of the court I began to recognize the depth of emotional pain and desperation of many of the families who came to court seeking help on behalf of their loved ones who were ill. I understood that to humanize justice, court proceedings needed to feel welcoming and hopeful. My goal was to create a sharp contrast to how court process typically was experienced by articulating a warm welcome and by explaining the concepts and principles of psychiatric rehabilitation in simple, easy-to-understand terms, whenever possible. The mission for a court of refuge would be to leverage the law to reach a therapeutic outcome. How I spoke and the way I described the mission of the court needed to be authentic, and the goal of decriminalization had to be demonstrated by words paired with judicial action.

According to the principles of therapeutic jurisprudence, it is the psychological forces of the court process that can "tip the scales" toward dignity and respect. From the perspective of procedural justice, the perception of fairness is what matters, and defendants must have the opportunity to share their lived experiences with the court so they feel that they have been heard. In terms of communication and court process, there is always a presumption of trauma, meaning that the court process is needed to support the restoration of personhood through the value of dignity. Therefore, the tone of my voice and language needed to reflect that value. An empathic tone coupled with a strength-based approach to recovery would be reaffirmed in continuous messaging by me: "If you want our help to engage in care—we will do everything we can do to support you."

I also understood that the courtroom needed to be a classroom. There are so many myths to shatter about mental illness, such as the stigma and the shame that can accompany a diagnosis of mental illness. It was imperative to learn about people's lives in order to humanize the court process. This was done by asking basic questions, such as "What did you want to be when you were young?" "What are your dreams? Did you go to school?" Through this process, we were subtly putting centuries of discrimination and institutional bias on trial. In a therapeutic court, traditional formalities that have historically defined the court process needed to be recast to humanize justice, not just for the court participants but for the attorneys, court staff, and the community at large.

Whereas typical courtrooms command a certain degree of awe and respect for traditions steeped in archaic forms of address and formality, the mental health court placed its judge on the level of a provider of human services. The unprecedented informality was often the key factor that allowed our clients to truly divulge their histories, which in turn made it possible for the court to link them to the services they desperately needed.

I scanned the courtroom to see who was present. I noticed that the court was filled with new referrals, family members, and court observers. I was particularly interested in a petite woman I saw while entering the courtroom. She appeared to be upset, and I asked the deputy if he would escort her up to the bench. I learned that her name was Ellen Boyd, and she was here on behalf of her son, Hayden, who had been arrested for allegedly stealing several packs of batteries from a local pharmacy.

"Hayden is a good boy," she said, almost in a whisper.

"I know this is difficult," I said, "but we are going to help you."

In truth, I shared her emotional pain. I could tell from the arrest paperwork that Hayden was young and struggling. Hayden was twenty-five years old and had been diagnosed with schizophrenia. He had been transferred by the judge in the first appearance court to the Broward County Mental Health Court. According to Rule 3.130 of the Florida Rules of Criminal Procedure, every person arrested must be taken to a judicial officer within twenty-four hours of arrest to be advised of the charges and to make legal findings. When the Broward County Mental Health Court was established, first appearance court was identified as the earliest point in the arrest process to intervene and identify people with mental illness who may qualify for the mental health court and who require psychiatric screening, triage, and swift diversion from the jail system.[1]

Today, Hayden was returning to court after having been transferred to the mental health court about a week earlier. Hayden had been clinically screened and assessed, and the clinical screening indicated that Hayden would meet the legal criteria for involuntary civil commitment. An emergency order for transportation had been entered by the court.

Hayden appeared confused and in a daze as he entered the courtroom in shackles and handcuffs. He had not posted bond, and technically he was still considered to be in the care and custody of the jail. Because he was no longer dressed in a jail jumpsuit, everyone wondered: Is Hayden a prisoner or a patient? The shackles and handcuffs said "prisoner," but what he was wearing said "patient."

I took a deep breath and grabbed a tissue in case I needed one. These moments are always very difficult for me.

I asked Hayden's mother if she needed a tissue. She shook her head no and proceeded to bury her face in a handkerchief and sob. When she recovered, she said, "I can't bear to see my son in handcuffs. He is a good boy."

"Of course he is," I said. Then I told her that he was going home. "It is important to talk about what we need to do next so Hayden can get well and live a meaningful life."

Mrs. Boyd raised her head and listened as I began to explain the basics of mental health recovery, engagement, and treatment planning. I grabbed the nearest legal pad and turned it over to the cardboard side, where I always begin my simplified explanation of the importance of person-centered treatment planning, which is so central to the work of the mental health court.

I drew a pie chart with several slices and placed a stick figure in the middle of the pie. I marked the first slice "medications" and another slice "talk therapy." The third slice represented psychosocial services, such as day treatment, community case management, and peer support. The fourth slice included nutrition and fitness; the fifth slice, enrichment activities such as favorite social activities and hobbies, creative pursuits, and spirituality. The sixth slice was for goals related to education, work, and career development.

Every time I near the end of this demonstration, I point to the stick figure in the center of the pie to emphasize that the treatment and service plan is person-centered. I did this for Hayden and his mother. Making a circle with my arms, I said, "This means your treatment plan is intended to wrap around you and evolve to meet the wants and needs of a person's vision of recovery."[2] Each time I describe a person-centered plan, I emphasize that everyone's path to recovery is unique and every individual has the potential to recover.

Instinctively, I leaned forward in my chair.

"You need to know, Mrs. Boyd," I said with conviction, "that people can and do recover from serious mental illness, like they recover from physical illnesses. Hayden has great strengths and gifts. With patience, and an abiding belief in recovery, these strengths will guide his recovery."

Mrs. Boyd nodded in agreement, even though she was visibly overwhelmed.

It is fair to say that the pie charts I make in court to demonstrate person-centered care are makeshift and simple. In fact, each time I go through this exercise (which takes several minutes) I joke that I should use a pre-made demonstration poster. But of course, that would be too easy and too impersonal.

Despite my misgivings about the simplicity of my explanation, I cling to the view that my spontaneity and intensity communicate caring and inspire hope. Perhaps it is my passion or how I abruptly rummage through my stacks of papers to locate a legal pad? In a court that applies therapeutic jurisprudence not necessarily what a judge says but how the court process is experienced is what remains with clients and their families after the court session has ended.

Often, when I draw the chart, I notice the other defendants sitting in the jury box lean in to listen to my remarks about recovery. I ask them, "Did you understand what I was saying?"

Usually they smile and enthusiastically nod their heads yes. A few may even give me a thumbs-up.

"Look to the future," I tell them. "There is no reason why all of you cannot transcend whatever is happening in order to live a positive and productive life." I often refer to the Adverse Childhood Experience (ACE) Study, which focuses on the consequences of unresolved trauma and victimization.[3] The ACE Study is one of the largest scientific research studies in the United States that has provided evidence of the relationship between adverse childhood experience, chronic medical disease, and negative social consequences.[4] I began applying the ACE Study in the court process within the first few years of the court's existence. It was clear to me that when one understood the evidence base and data surrounding the consequences of unresolved trauma and victimization, court participants could better understand the "why" behind their poor choices, unhealthy behaviors, and bad decision-making.

The ACE Study, which started in 1985, was conducted by Kaiser Permanente and the Centers for Disease Control to determine why people enrolled in a Kaiser Permanente obesity clinic were dropping out, notwithstanding their success in the program. The initial findings of surveys led the researchers, Dr. Vincent Felitti and Dr. Robert Anda, to the conclusion that a majority of the 286 people surveyed had experienced childhood sexual abuse.[5] From 1995 to 1997, the study expanded to include over 17,000 middle-class members of Kaiser Permanente's San Diego Care Program.[6] The results revealed that adverse childhood experiences play a profound role in the future of one's health and quality of life. The higher one's ACE score the greater the risk one would be affected by chronic medical illness, including mental illnesses such as depression, anxiety, and substance abuse.

The ACE Study developed a framework of ten ACE "events," including three types of abuse (physical, sexual, and emotional) and seven types of family dysfunction (mother treated child violently, substance abuse in household, mental illness in household, parental separation or divorce, criminal member of household, emotional neglect, physical neglect).[7] The ACE Study and its findings are used in many courts throughout the United States, including family law courts, juvenile courts, and dependency courts.

As in all matters of public health, prevention and early intervention for children are critical. The economic costs of childhood maltreatment in America across all institutional systems, including criminal justice, totaled $124 billion in 2012.[8] In mental health court, the information surrounding childhood maltreatment and the ways adverse childhood experiences often lead to risky behavior, substance abuse, and justice involvement is often, actually, welcome news. This is because for many individuals who come before the mental health court, it is the first time they realize that their attempts to fix their problems were not adequate on their own, but that through a therapeutic approach they could begin to heal from traumatic experiences that have followed them like a black cloud.

I let them know that everyone has something to recover from. Usually, several defendants look at each other with approval. This is when they "get" it. They are engaged and eager to affirm what they are hearing.

In addition to the educational value of my pie charts and discussions with clients, I have found that these discussions go a long way toward promoting human dignity. In the course of my career I have always believed it is important for the men and women involved in the criminal justice system to be informed, to know that the science behind trauma and treatment aids people's ability to connect the dots, to be advocates for themselves, and to appreciate the root causes of human behavior, including their own. In this part of mental health court, we usually talk about the social determinants of population health and disparities in health care that may have contributed to their involvement with the judicial system in the first place.

Social determinants of health such as poverty, unequal access to health care, lack of education, unemployment, racism, and adverse childhood experiences and trauma are drivers that can lead to incarceration. According to the data, poor people, especially people of color, face a greater likelihood of being arrested for minor offenses than other Americans.[9] These intersections give rise to the need to implement mental health screenings and interventions for children to prevent the worsening of adverse childhood experiences, and they are essential to the promotion of public health, public safety, and social justice. According to the Bureau of Justice Statistics, in 2016, half of all jail inmates reported having a chronic medical condition such as cancer, high blood pressure, diabetes, asthma, or heart problems. More than 40 percent reported suffering from a mental health disorder such as manic depression, bipolar disorder, schizophrenia, and anxiety.[10] More than half of jail inmates without mental health problems were dependent on or abused alcohol or drugs, and more than three-quarters of jail inmates met criteria for co-occurring mental health issues and substance use dependency or abuse in 2002.[11] As for women in the criminal justice system, several sources, including the Center for American Progress, have reported that 85 to 90 percent of women who are incarcerated or under community corrections supervision in the US have a history of being victims of domestic violence and sexual abuse, and suffer from a substance abuse disorder.[12]

There is no doubt that mental health is essential to overall health, and education is vital.

I often continue my courtroom lecture for a few more minutes, sounding more like a professor than a judge. During moments like this, I ask the courtroom, "What is the relevance of the question 'What happened to you?'" For many, it offers a point of beginning for self-reflection and the realization that personal restoration is possible. Research reveals that many people seek personal solutions to emotional pain. The problem is that most people opt for a band-aid approach, for quick fixes such as self-medication with alcohol or drugs and sensation- or thrill-seeking behaviors.

"Often, personal solutions may seem helpful but can lead to negative outcomes," I say. I cite the work of Dr. Steven Gold, a professor of psychology and a national expert on trauma, to encourage mental health court participants "that healing from trauma is possible."[13] I offer handouts about the ACE Study for those who are interested. We usually end the session talking about strategic goal setting and about taking a restorative approach. Once we understand the science and research behind trauma and recovery, we all have a responsibility as adults to work toward recovery from a therapeutic approach versus quick fixes—which only exacerbate the problems.

Each time I engage with the courtroom this way, I think to myself, *This is what a therapeutic courtroom feels like.* Every day, I can discuss the promotion of public health and mental health in a criminal justice context with an audience whose members need to hear it the most. In addition to linking these subjects with discussions about personal accountability and individual choices, we talk about conflict resolution and the promotion of peace. These are high-altitude discussions, which at the very least offer constructive food for thought and at best can ignite transformative change.

During these moments, which sometimes feel more like an episode of *Oprah* than a courtroom, there is often laughter when spontaneous comments emanate from the jury box or gallery. I often ask, "What did you want to be when you were little? What was your vision? It's never too late to make that pivot."

You never know what someone will say.

The positive discourse in the courtroom shifts the energy, and feelings of optimism emerge. Once a defendant said, "Thank you,

Judge Lerner-Wren. No one has ever talked to us like this before."
This is the power of therapeutic jurisprudence.

If a judge has the desire to relate to her defendants from an
authentic human level, then the essence of humanizing justice, I
hope, has begun to be realized.

During the educational portion of the docket, legal and clinical
staff are busy reviewing case statuses and calling community providers to ask about bed accessibility and community placements.
It is fair to say that it's helpful to have a larger courtroom to accommodate the clinical screening and problem-solving activities
of the mental health court, which require care coordination and
system navigation. It is important to note that although the style
of judging and the informal atmosphere in a therapeutic court are
different than in a traditional court, the courtroom is the same.
For example, when one enters my assigned courtroom, there are six
rows of benches on either side of the public gallery. There is a jury
box with two rows of six high-back leather chairs. One feature of
the courtroom is a large painting the size of a mural, contributed
by a retired public defender, Fred Goldstein, in 2007, that faces the
jury box. It commemorates the mental health court's tenth anniversary. I named the painting *Horizons* because of its sprawling landscape of sky blue and pale green, expressing a vision of peace and
well-being. Finally, facing the bench are two podiums, for legal argument, and two tables, one each for the state prosecuting attorney
and for the defense attorney.

Since the mental health court's inception, I have been fortunate
to have the support of experts in the field of mental health law and
therapeutic jurisprudence (TJ). David B. Wexler describes therapeutic jurisprudence as "the study of the role of the law as a therapeutic
agent. It focuses on the law's impact on emotional life and well-
being. The science of therapeutic jurisprudence is a perspective
that the law is *a social force* which produces behaviors and consequences."[14] I called on Wexler and Bruce J. Winick, both law professors, and Michael L. Perlin, a professor of disabilities rights law

and human rights, to ask whether they would be willing to act as consultants on court process. They all graciously agreed. The law reform science of TJ was already being applied in other problem-solving courts, such as drug courts and domestic violence courts. The revolutionary concept that courts have the potential to heal was a perfect fit for Broward's newest addition to the array of problem-solving courts.

I was ready to call the next case when I heard someone begin to yell from the back of the courtroom. Two jail deputies escorted a young, intellectually disabled man to the front of the court. Handcuffed and distraught, Joseph Henry, a twenty-four-year-old man dressed in street clothes, was a client of Florida's Agency for Persons with Disabilities (APD). He had seen his independent support coordinator, Samantha, sitting in the gallery. "Sam! Sam!" he called.

Joseph lived in an APD group home in the community. He had been arrested for loitering at a convenience store. I immediately called Sam to the bench. I introduced myself and thanked her for her service. I proudly shared with her that as a former public guardian for Broward County, I was responsible for the health, welfare, and safety of many adults with developmental disabilities—a uniquely gratifying role.

I asked her whether she was permitted to transport Joseph back to his group home. She said she could.

"Fantastic," I said. "Perhaps you could go over and let Joseph know he will be going home with you in a few minutes?"

I watched as the two spoke like old friends. Joseph became calmer. I took another deep breath and thought about what could have happened to him in a jail setting. If his demeanor entering the courtroom was any indication, Joseph would have felt trapped and would have exhibited behaviors that prison staff could have mistaken for aggression or violence. Correctional officers responsible for Joseph's care and custody, who are not trained to appreciate his intellectual challenges, might have misinterpreted his inability to follow simple instructions and responded punitively. Such a response could easily escalate, causing Joseph to feel threatened and act out. This would subject Joseph to disciplinary action, which could include seclusion or restraint, possible use of excessive force, or being placed in solitary confinement.

The next person on the docket was Roger, the first case heard by the mental health court. Greg Forster, the mental health court clinician, on loan from Henderson Behavioral Health Center in Broward County, told me that Roger was now ready for his case to be called. Recently discharged from the psychiatric receiving facility, Roger was not alone in court—his parents had come with him.

Greg began the hearing by introducing Roger's parents. He informed me that Roger had gone missing for several years and had been homeless. His engagement with the court had led to his reunion with his family. An older couple, Roger's parents were from Central America and spoke little English. I asked my clerk, Digna Gonzalez, if she would help translate for them.

Roger's hair was cut, and for the first time, we could see his face. He was nicely dressed in a long-sleeved collared shirt and jeans. He was smiling and happy to be back with his family. Roger's father thanked the court and wanted to let me know that they had known that something was wrong with Roger, but did not know what to do to help him.

As my clerk helped Roger's parents speak to us, I learned that Roger had been raised in South Florida and had become ill in his late teens. We talked about the mission of the court, and I appointed legal counsel on his behalf.

I let Roger's parents know that what happened to their son and the disintegration of their family were the reasons this court was established. To underscore the importance of defendants like Roger, I added, "What you experienced is a social injustice, which must end." Then I explained Roger's constitutional right to challenge in a trial the disorderly conduct that had resulted from the disturbance in the convenience store, and I emphasized that participation in the mental health court is voluntary.

"I want to stay in the mental health court," Roger said.

Greg indicated that Roger's discharge plan called for Roger to live at a residential supportive housing program, close to his family's home. I established for the record that I had agreed to Roger's plan upon notification from the hospital that Roger was well enough to be released and then had issued an order for Roger to go directly to his housing program. With treatment and a safe place to live near his family, Roger was doing much better. He was soft-spoken but told the court that he would be attending day treatment and spending time with his family.

"I . . . I would also like to go back to school," he said quietly.

I was thrilled, and the entire courtroom broke out in applause. We couldn't help it. The applause was as much for Roger as it was to acknowledge that the mental health court was working. I congratulated Roger on his achievements and asked him if it would be OK for him to come back to court to let us know how he was progressing on his discharge plan goals.

He said it would be.

We gave him a future court date to review competency issues. Under Florida law, when a person is charged with a misdemeanor offense and found by the judge to be "incompetent to proceed to trial," the judge has no legal authority to forensically commit that individual for purposes of competency restoration—that is, commit her or him to a state hospital, jail, or prison, like persons charged with a felony offense.[15] A defendant is incompetent to proceed to trial "if that individual does not have sufficient present ability to consult with their lawyer with a reasonable degree of rational understanding of the proceedings against him/her."[16] The issue of forensic commitment has emerged as a serious problem in the state of Florida due to spiraling costs associated with the objective of competency restoration for purposes of standing trial.

In 2015, the *Tampa Bay Times–Herald Tribune* ran a series of investigative reports on Florida's mental health institutions. In one of the stories, it was said that after paying for months of "competency training," patients are released, often back into the local jail system. As they wait for their cases to be scheduled, they relapse, and the entire forensic commitment process is repeated, until that person is released, as in the case of Aaron Wynn, with no place to live and no support—leaving individuals and families desperate for mental health services.[17] Further, although many correctional officers and personnel do their best to meet the needs of the mentally ill population, there have been allegations of abuse and neglect of inmates, such as in the case of Aaron Wynn.[18] In 2015, Human Rights Watch reported that an estimated four hundred thousand inmates with mental disabilities and intellectual disorders are held in US jails, prisons, and forensic hospitals. According to HRW surveys, staff shortages, overcrowding, inadequate training for staff in techniques for deescalating conflict and trauma, and a lack of rehabilitative programming can contribute to incidents of punitive disciplinary actions, which may include excessive use of solitary confinement, seclusion, restraint, physical and psychological abuse, and the denial of food or medical care.[19]

The presiding judge's goal is not only to divert people with mental illness and co-occurring disorders out of the prison system and to community-based care, but also to prevent people from languishing in jail or from being trapped in a revolving door of arrest cycles. Under Florida law, persons charged with a misdemeanor offense who have been found by a judge to be incompetent to proceed to trial are subject to case dismissal at twelve months from the date of the order after a hearing that finds that there has been no change in competency status.[20]

I anticipated that Roger's case would ultimately be dismissed.

The marathon session continued and the public defender advised me that several of her clients wanted to challenge their charges by way of trial—that is, they wanted their cases to go to trial. After private consultations with the public defender, her clients decided to ask to opt out of participating in the mental health court. After all, the mental health court is voluntary and offers a problem-solving treatment, not a traditional trial. Many individuals are interested in participating in a therapeutic court in exchange for avoiding the risk of sanction, such as probation or jail. In this sense, the court offers a positive alternative to the traditional court process. On the other hand, those individuals who desire to exercise their constitutional rights to have their day in court may simply request to transfer out of the mental health court, and we let them know that the door remains open. I immediately signed a transfer order to have these individuals docketed in their regularly assigned criminal divisions.

Then I received the "all clear" from my deputy that Hayden was ready for release, which meant he could be released from the courtroom and did not need to return to jail for processing. I asked Hayden's mother to return to the bench and reminded her about how important it is to follow up with Hayden's discharge plan. I asked my judicial assistant to give his mother a written safety plan, which included important telephone numbers such as that of the Henderson Mobile Crisis Unit and other crisis hotlines of local community supports.

Currently, every court participant receives a mental health court safety plan including the telephone number for the National Suicide Prevention Lifeline and other contact information for crisis response and resiliency planning.[21] These precautions are necessary in Florida, which ranks forty-ninth in mental health funding in the country.[22] This is a deplorable circumstance, given that Florida is the third most populous state; hundreds of thousands of Floridians lack health insurance or Medicaid.[23] In fact, the state of mental health across the United States is in shambles. The lack of sufficient funding and investment in statewide mental health care delivery systems that are accessible, affordable, and recovery-oriented has led to crisis for individuals and families across our nation. What policymakers fail to realize is that according to the data one in five Americans (adults and children) suffers from a mental illness at some time in their lives.[24] The negative and collateral consequences of untreated mental illness, according to the National Alliance on Mental Illness, includes absenteeism, worsening health conditions, family erosion, homelessness, substance abuse and addiction, crime, incarceration, and suicide. From an economic perspective, untreated mental illness costs America $193.2 billion annually.[25]

In 1999, two years after the start of the Broward County's Mental Health Court, US Surgeon General David Satcher released the landmark *Surgeon General's Report on Mental Health*.[26] Satcher described a mental health field "plagued by disparities in the availability of and access to its services." He spoke of forty-four million Americans without health insurance and the fact that "we have allowed stigma and hopelessness to erect barriers to care—and [now we have] declared it is time to take them down."

As I thought about Hayden and his mother, I'm reminded of the words and the vision of Dr. Satcher for our nation. For the entire session, Hayden, still shackled, had stood quietly before the court as we waited for his paperwork to be processed.

It took only minute, but to me, seeing what happened next always feels like a miracle. The shackles and handcuffs were removed, and Hayden, now free, wrapped his arms around his mother, embracing her. The vision of the end of criminalization of people with mental illness in America comes to life in this moment.

CHAPTER 3

Punishing Loss

In her early thirties, Kathryn Steeves was married with three children and lived in a spacious five-bedroom house in the western part of Broward County. She had purchased the house herself after working for fifteen years as a restaurant manager—an accomplishment that she took great pride in. But with the unexpected collapse of her marriage and mounting financial pressures, the stress Kathryn was under became unmanageable. At the time of the divorce, although both she and her husband were working, money was tight. As conflicts over child support intensified, Kathryn's mental health rapidly declined.

Kathryn conceded, "I was an emotional mess." Suffering from severe panic attacks and depression that doctors would later diagnose as symptoms of bipolar disorder, Kathryn's perception of her life took a dark turn.

One night, in the middle of a psychological crisis, Kathryn walked out the door, down the street, and away from her home. She became a homeless person. "It just felt like the world caved in," she said. "I never considered that I may have been suffering from a mental illness."

For more than two and a half years, she struggled to adapt to life on the streets. Kathryn always strived to do her best. While homeless, she worked to build relationships and sought out people who could offer her food or a place to sleep. Kathryn still cannot explain why she never considered returning home, and she barely recalls the day she walked into a novelty shop in a South Florida mall and stuffed five harmonicas into her bag.

"I don't get it," she said. "I had never played a harmonica in my life. The only thing I remember is the day I appeared in mental health court."

"Why is that?" I asked.

"Because it was the first time I realized I had lost everything," she said.

According to a report written for the American College of Obstetricians and Gynecologists, "Women and families represent the fastest growing segment of the homeless population."[1] Studies reveal that 84 percent of homeless families are headed by women.[2] These women often choose homelessness over domestic violence and sexual violence—in fact, 20 to 50 percent of all homeless women and children become homeless because they were fleeing a violent situation at home.[3] African American families are disproportionately represented among the homeless population, making up 43 percent of homeless families.[4]

The committee's report emphasizes that the lack of healthcare represents a major risk for women and families, with 73 percent of homeless individuals reporting at least one unmet health need. These needs often include medical, surgical, mental health, vision, or dental care or prescription needs.[5] From an intersectional and criminal justice perspective, the committee found that substance abuse can be both a cause and a result of homelessness and can co-occur with mental illness.[6] According to the data, 30 percent of individuals who are chronically homeless have mental health conditions and an estimated 50 percent have co-occurring substance abuse disorders.[7]

In the late 1990s, the number of justice-involved women had increased dramatically.[8] By 2000, the figure had risen to more than one million.[9] According to the National Resource Center on Justice Involved Women, "Women's experiences within and outside the criminal justice system are markedly different from justice-involved men, and their needs are unique." Women's pathways into the criminal justice system, like Kathryn Steeves, are best understood in the context of relationships and are linked to past experiences of trauma and victimization, poverty, mental illness and substance abuse.[10] During a mental health crisis, women are more unlikely than men to seek mental health care and thus place themselves at a higher risk for justice system involvement. This is why an estimated 31 percent of women who are arrested for low-level crime have a serious mental health condition.[11] For many of the women who appear in the mental health court who have been exposed to trauma and victimization, the motivation to engage in mental health or substance abuse treatment is enhanced by the therapeutic approach, which is responsive and culturally sensitive to the unique needs of women.[12]

Lilly was a hard-working stay-at-home mom. Her husband was an accountant, and they seemed to have it all: a happy marriage, a beautiful home, and lovely children. Lilly had always lived a natural life; she did not believe in wearing makeup and was mindful of nutrition, adhering to a strict vegetarian diet. Or, this was true until Lilly's postpartum depression hit and became increasingly debilitating.

Over time, her conduct became more bizarre and unpredictable. At the pinnacle of her odd behavior, Lilly was charged with a misdemeanor offense of violation of a restraining order and was not able to post bond. As I reviewed her court file, I discovered that a family judge had issued a "stay away" order, which prohibited Lilly from returning to her former home to see her children. Despite the order, she returned anyway.

According to her husband she was not making sense and was delusional. She would leave the home for extended periods of time without notifying her husband of her whereabouts, leaving the children alone. She was staying up all hours of the night. He indicated that he did not feel it was safe to leave the children in her care.

Her husband appeared in court on her behalf. He was soft-spoken and stoic, even when he said, "As Lilly got worse, I had no choice but to file for divorce and seek custody of the children." Lilly was arrested and charged for the misdemeanor crime of violating an order of protection, as she was ordered to stay away from the family home where her children lived with her ex-husband. She was unable to post bond.

According to her husband, Lilly had refused to seek mental health treatment. He was concerned about the welfare of their children. He told Janis Blenden, a licensed clinical social worker who served as the in-court clinician, that Lilly had been hospitalized numerous times, only to be released within seventy-two hours because she refused medications. But it was her refusal to stay away from her own home that brought her case to the attention of the mental health court.

She had been referred to the mental health court by her division judge. Lilly's public defender argued that the family home was the only one her client had ever known and she wanted to be with her children. As presiding judge, I have always maintained that every individual appearing in the mental health court be represented by a public defender if the individual could not afford to retain private counsel. Given the high prevalence of homelessness among adult inmates in jail, most people in the court (15.3 percent) cannot afford a lawyer and are represented by a public defender who is specially assigned to the mental health court.[13] Lilly's public defender also argued that given Lilly's mental health condition, it was doubtful her client understood that there was a restraining order in place, and she had no intention of violating the restraining order.

I was shocked at Lilly's appearance when she came before me in mental health court. She had been chronically homeless, and as a result, she was rail-thin and highly vulnerable. Janis screened Lilly. She had been hand-picked for this position because of her clinical experience, passion for recovery, and expertise in community resources. When the court was designed, I believed it was essential to have an experienced clinician embedded in the court process in order to effectively braid in psychosocial dialogues during criminal court hearings and to allow for spontaneous problem solving to expedite the diversionary process. As an excellent problem solver, Janis was highly skilled in service integration and creative treatment planning. I often joked that the more complex the problem, the better she performed. The court was also provided with a mental health court monitor, Bertha Smith, who was sought out for the position based on her expertise in housing for people with mental illness and cognitive disabilities. The court monitor is responsible for overseeing compliance of those individuals being followed by the court in the community. The monitor's duties are to report any problems or concerns to the court and generally to track the status of each case. Unfortunately, this position was defunded in 2008 as a result of budget cuts. The monitoring function was taken over by Janis, who has always maintained that our streamlined court staff works efficiently because of the strength of its relationships.

When Janis concluded her screening, she recommended that Lilly be sent to the hospital to be evaluated for psychiatric treatment and stabilization. I issued the emergency transportation order and hoped that Lilly would be admitted.

I did not realize it then, but there were obvious similarities between Lilly's and Kathryn's situations. Both women's pathways to jail were largely due to homelessness and untreated mental illness and trauma, and both had lost custody of their children.

Each in her own way demonstrated that the challenges and individual needs of women are distinct and complex. Additionally, both Kathryn and Lilly faced a vexing problem unique to women in need of help: a lack of gender-specific services and housing for women who suffer from mental illness, substance abuse, and the residue of trauma.

Kathryn had been in custody, homeless, and unable to post the $25 bond (a customary amount imposed by a judge for a minor petty theft arrest) when she appeared in mental health court. Although the first appearance judge had agreed to release Kathryn on her own recognizance under pretrial supervision, Kathryn had nowhere to go—no place to live. Recognizing the impracticality of this order, Kathryn's pretrial release officer referred her to the mental health court.

When Kathryn appeared in court, more than anything she wanted to regain legal custody of her children. She was highly motivated to engage in treatment and she enthusiastically embraced her mental health care in order to get well and rebuild her life. Her assigned pretrial release officer was well versed on the court, and she knew that a residential program had recently been dedicated to the court for defendants who were homeless. Located on the Howard Forman Campus in the City of Pembroke Pines, "the Cottages in the Pines" opened in 1998 as a twenty-four-bed transitional residential facility that answered the need for a dedicated housing resource for the mental health court. The program was intended for individuals who were homeless or at risk of homelessness and provided a needed resource in order to break arrest cycles and allow for treatment engagement and stabilization in the community.[14]

In Kathryn's case, Bertha Smith, the court monitor, called the director of the Cottages to confirm that a bed for Kathryn was available. He told her they had available space. The court ordered Kathryn to the Cottages to begin her journey to recovery. Along with other residents at the Cottages, Kathryn was scheduled to return to court in a month so the court could monitor her progress.

The current state of gender-specific services has not gone unnoticed by researchers and advocates. In recent years, several universities and nonprofits have come together in an effort to address this glaring gap in services. One advocate in Florida is Lenore E. Walker, the pioneer researcher of battered-woman syndrome and coordinator of the concentration in forensic psychology at the College of Psychology at Nova Southeastern University, in Broward County.

In 1998, Dr. Walker stepped up to the podium in my courtroom and introduced herself. I had never met Dr. Walker before, but I certainly knew of her leadership in research on domestic violence and on gender and the cycle of violence.[15] She told those in the courtroom that the president of Nova Southeastern University,

Ray F. Ferraro Jr., had asked her to let me know that the university would provide any available resources I would need to support the court. I was overwhelmed; the court had no budget and had received no grants.

Within a few years, however, through the US Department of Justice, Dr. Walker and I applied for a Criminal Justice Mental Health and Community Collaborative Grant, a federal grant intended to promote jail diversion; our application was dedicated to gender-specific services for women. These grants are highly competitive because a wide range of institutions and nonprofits are eligible to apply for them. Despite the large number of applicants, the grant was awarded to Nova Southeastern University in collaboration with the mental health court to serve women with serious mental illness and co-occurring disorders. The program targeted women who were arrested on nonviolent misdemeanor charges. Under the grant, we received an estimated $50,000 for one year; the grant was then extended for eighteen months. It was to be used to establish a comprehensive mental health and drug treatment day program for justice-involved women who were participants in Broward's Mental Health Court.[16]

The university rented a 4,500-square-foot building within walking distance of the courthouse. It was a fitting space to occupy as its previous occupant had been Legal Aid Services of Broward County, dedicated to fighting for the legal rights of marginalized populations.

The grant allowed us to establish the South Florida Medical Corrections Options Program. Called Options for short, the program was hailed by the community as a needed resource to fill gaps in mental health services for women and their families.[17] At the time, Broward County had one long-term housing program for women with mental illness and co-occurring substance disorders and one short-term treatment program. Over 30 percent of women involved in the criminal justice system have at least one serious mental illness, but they also have children at home. The goal of Options was to break arrest cycles and to promote healthy living and wellness, and it represented an important new resource not only for the court but for the women in need of services in Broward County.[18]

For Lilly, however, an outpatient program such as Options was not a possibility. She required more intensive services, evidenced by her current condition: after her first appearance in the mental health court, Lilly was back in jail. The doctor at the local psychiatric receiving facility found that she did not meet the criteria for involuntary civil commitment. We were back at square one.

My office scheduled her to return to court immediately. We needed to regroup and form a new game plan. Lilly's ex-husband had confirmed that Lilly was diagnosed with a nonspecific delusional disorder. At the follow-up hearing, Lilly was adamant that she have the right to return to her home. She maintained her position that she had a right to be with her children no matter how many times her public defender tried to explain that the family law judge who was presiding over the child custody issues had ordered her not to return to her former home. Even though I am a judge, when I preside over mental health court cases, I do not have the legal authority to overrule the presiding family law judge, who is also a circuit court judge and whose authority is superior to that of county court judge under Article V of the Constitution of the State of Florida.

I informed Lilly that if she returned to the property, she could not only be re-arrested, but she could conceivably be subject to contempt proceedings in the family court.

Lilly dug in. "I have a right to see my children and to return to my home," she said.

Lilly's needs were unique and her situation, dire. I was concerned that if she returned to the property, existing tensions would escalate. Any way one analyzed the situation, Lilly was at risk. Janis agreed: Lilly was highly vulnerable and at risk on the streets. If her criminal case was transferred back to a traditional court, her options would likely be limited to either an extended jail stay or release of Lilly and homelessness. Janis did not believe that Lilly would stay at a homeless shelter, even if ordered to do so by the court.

The negotiations continued for hours. I offered Lilly a bed at the Cottages. She would be safe there. I was confident that the other residents would support her. Always optimistic, I thought that at least she would be part of a therapeutic community, which in turn could lead to her engagement in treatment. To stay at the Cottages, Lilly had to agree to take her medications.

"All right," Lilly finally said, after listening to my explanation. "But I have conditions."

Lilly refused to take medications.

I thought we were making progress. Then, she changed her mind.

Around and around we went about the fact that she would not take medications and believed she had a right to return to her property. Finally, I realized the issue of medication was a barrier to her agreeing to go the Cottages. We were getting nowhere.

I asked Janis to call Dr. Tim Ludwig, the manager of in-custody behavioral services at the Broward County Sheriff's Office since 2002, to inquire if the Henderson Behavioral Health Center would allow Lilly to reside at the Cottages even if she chose not to take medications. Dr. Ludwig indicated she could. Slowly, other obstacles began to fade.

Finally, Lilly agreed to give the Cottages a chance.

I drafted the order to have Lilly transported to the Cottages the next day. I included the condition "no return to the property" in the order. Thankfully, Lilly agreed to comply. The court would monitor her progress. I prayed silently that she would stay there. For Lilly, there were no other mental health services. There was no plan B.

CHAPTER 4

The Raging
Voice of Dignity

"Quiet please," the court deputy bellowed. "Court has begun."

The mental health court docket is sandwiched in between morning and afternoon sessions of my regular county criminal division and there is never a spare moment to waste. Each day it is imperative that I give every defendant the time they need. I have learned from Lilly and so many others that there is no telling how complex an individual's case may be or what may occur while we are trying to find the most appropriate solution to a defendant's request in mental health court.

"Judge Lerner-Wren." A frail female voice traveled over the heads of other court attendees. The defendant, named Marian, sat in the first high-back leather chair in the jury box, closest to my bench.

"Yes," I said in a calm voice.

Marian was handcuffed to the high-back chair. She was a tall woman with shoulder-length brown hair that was partially pulled back while some strands hung loosely around her face. I thought to myself that whatever Marian has been going through, she looked as if she was having a very rough time.

Today, several representatives of the Broward County chapter of the National Alliance on Mental Illness (NAMI) were present as court advocates for Marian. NAMI members Joanne Neagus, Evelyn Miller, Pastor Barbara Shaw, and Bernice Cooper, regular fixtures in the court, were here to lend support to the distraught woman in the jury box. This was not unusual: Broward NAMI is a major referral source for the mental health court and has offered advocacy services during court proceedings since the court's inception. In truth, although the court is dedicated to Aaron Wynn, it is also considered a gift to Broward's NAMI families and mental health consumers due to NAMI's integral role in advocating for the creation of the court. Many NAMI members met with the former Broward County chief judge, Dale Ross, and shared with him their experiences with the mental health system. Their insights helped to highlight the need for a specialized court.

Marian, who suffered from depression and co-occurring substance use disorder, demonstrated this need distinctly. She was chronically homeless and had been arrested for possession of drug paraphernalia.

"Judge," she cried, "I am so ashamed! Look at this—look—I'm in shackles!" Marian lifted her feet up and placed them on top of the jury box so everyone could see the shackles around her ankles.

Her display was shocking, but I said nothing in reply. Everyone in the courtroom was stunned silent and knew better than to interrupt her.

"Judge Lerner-Wren," she sobbed, "I am not a bad person. I am sick, and this is how our nation treats its citizens who are ill. This isn't right!"

I hesitated to speak. Instead, I chose to remain silent, to allow her to continue her remarks while showing the shackles on her legs, which dangled over the jury bench. I hoped that this demonstration would somehow allow her to release some of her emotional pain and humiliation.

After letting her words weigh on the silence, Marian began again: "I just don't know how our elected officials and policymakers can allow people with mental illness to be arrested instead of pro-viding us care." I glanced over at a group of Nova University grad students in the courtroom and wondered how they were reacting to this spontaneous "testimonial of shame." Every day, doctoral stu-dents were embedded in the first appearance court and were present in the mental health courtroom to assist with screenings as well as to act as clinical advisors to the court.

Marian began to speak in the third person, between intermittent sobs. All that we could hear are the words "It's so dehumanizing," uttered between sharply intaken breaths.

When she composed herself, she said, "I just wanted to tell you that." With that, Marian lifted her shackled legs and placed her feet back on the floor of the jury box.

Now it was my turn. I thought carefully about my words. A primary goal of the court is to promote dignity and the restoration of personhood. These values and actionable goals are embedded in every facet of the court process through a fidelity to therapeutic jus-tice. It is never easy to allow myself to be vulnerable in my role as a judge. Yet, my ability to build trust and promote dignity depends upon my ability to be authentic.

"Marian," I said gently with respect and empathy. "I have no words, other than to say that you are right."

Then I decided to share a personal experience that directly re-lated to the dehumanization she had so poignantly described and demonstrated.

"I remember many years ago, when I was a young lawyer and working with people with disabilities, I learned for the first time about the trend known as the criminalization of people with mental illness. I was shocked, and I thought to myself that it couldn't be— not in America. Yet, this is where we are, and this court is going to do everything it can to help you get the care you need so you will not have to suffer the degradation and the humiliation of arrest again."

My comments, while heartfelt, were the abridged version of an experience that for me was actually more dramatic and memorable. When I first heard about the criminalization of people with mental illness, I was a young lawyer who was just learning about disability rights. It was 1992, and I was attending a mental health conference where hundreds of other lawyers, judges, and mental health advocates filled the grand ballroom of the hotel for the plenary session on mental health and criminal justice. The presenter, a researcher whose presentation outlined the overrepresentation of people with serious mental illness in our nation's jails and prisons, recounted the troubling demographics of American jailhouses.

The speaker explained the impact of the civil rights movement and the national policy shift to deinstitutionalization of the mentally ill—returning them to communities. He described the many factors that doomed President John F. Kennedy's vision for the Community Mental Health Act of 1963, where the network of state-run hospitals and institutions (referred to as asylums) would be largely replaced with a more socially inclusive community-based mental health system. This, the researcher underscored, never occurred, and thousands of people once hospitalized ended up on the streets and ultimately in jail. Many people were arrested for nuisance and quality-of-life types of crimes, such as trespassing, disorderly conduct, and panhandling. The result is known as the "criminalization of people with mental illness," a historic trend that, according to the law professor Michael L. Perlin, was based upon a hidden prejudice called "sanism," which, like racism, "pervaded western culture throughout history and is rooted across all social and governmental institutions, including our legal system."[1]

I recall that several years after the establishment of the mental health court, I sat down with the Broward County public defender, Howard Finkelstein, and asked him to describe his vision for the court when he proposed it to the members of Broward County's Criminal Justice and Mental Health Task Force. "Basically," Howard said, "judges aren't trained in mental health. Many judges don't know how to relate to someone with a mental illness. My vision was to establish a court that would not only promote the due process and constitutional rights of every individual, but a court in which the judge would see every person 'as deserving of respect, and do no harm.'"[2]

This is, of course, contrary to what I have witnessed during my tenure working in the disability rights field. What would Marian's display have elicited in any court but the mental health court? I have witnessed outright prejudice, stigmatization, and discrimination as the socially acceptable reactions to an encounter with mental illness—these are the reactions that Marian would have elicited. This matches the research, particularly by Perlin, who catalogued the many false assumptions that are made by society and the legal system in regard to those who live with mental disabilities. According to Perlin, these beliefs include stereotypes such as that people with mental disabilities are lazy, dangerous, emotionally unstable, erratic, and incapable of rational executive decision-making. In other words, there is a presumption that a person with a mental disability is incapable of making rational choices—or of even thinking as you or I do.[3]

"I'm going to make my own decisions?" Marian asked quietly.

"Yes," I said. "You always have. This time, those decisions will lead you to the life you want to live."

It wasn't shocking to me that she asked this kind of questions. After all, the criminalization of people with mental illness is by no means new; in fact, it has been a tried and true method of social control and management since the beginning of recorded history. Yet it was not called into question until March 28, 1841, the cold, windy day that Dorothea Lynde Dix paid a visit to the East Cambridge, Massachusetts, jail to teach a Bible study class to a group of prisoners.[4] It was a visit that would change history: Dorothea Dix discovered two indigent women with mental illness confined, shivering, in a dirty cage with no heat.[5] She knew something had to change.

That cold day in 1841 sparked Dix's quest for humanity and dignity for the mentally ill. It launched a forty-year research and advocacy campaign for what she hoped would become a solution to eliminate the criminalization of people with mental illness.[6] Dix advocated for compassionate care and treatment that would be delivered in hospitals, an approach that aligned with her Civil War experience. However, the model for which she advocated, a statewide network of large psychiatric institutions, was never quite realized.

Over one hundred years later, in January 1955, President Eisenhower delivered a speech, "Special Message to Congress Recommending a Health Program," which laid a strong foundation for President John F. Kennedy's initiative, when he urged Congress to expand healthcare insurance benefits.[7] Eisenhower outlined a comprehensive public health agenda that included new hospitals and an aggressive approach to mental health and enhanced participation in the World Health Organization of the United Nations to promote global cooperation and economic growth and to preempt the spread of communism.[8] This leads us to 1963 and the Community Mental Health Act, signed into law by JFK, whose promise also was never fulfilled owing to Kennedy's assassination, local resistance to community-based mental health centers being situated in residential areas, and to engagement in the Vietnam War.[9]

By the 1980s, a new wave of criminalization had begun. In addition to the traditional stigmatization of and discrimination against the mentally ill, people with mental health problems now were often additionally depicted as violent, dangerous, or frightening, a perception that became magnified due to increased homelessness and the involvement of law enforcement as more and more mentally ill people were deinstitutionalized. According to a report published in 2013, "As the lay public became exposed to a formally 'hidden segment of the population,' the stigma which led to the failure of the deinstitutionalization movement was reinforced and enhanced." In fact, the data show that people with serious mental illness are ten times as likely to be victimized as those who are not afflicted with a mental illness.[10]

By the 1990s, thousands of mentally ill people had been made homeless, and many were self-medicating with illegal street drugs and alcohol, which led them to commit quality-of-life offenses for behavioral symptoms related to their mental illness. This was when I, as a young lawyer, heard that people with mental illness were being incarcerated in America instead of being treated in community healthcare settings.

As I thought about this, I kept my attention on Marian. I could relate to how she felt. Even though we were two women in very different stations in life, there was commonality in our humanity and a shared moral view of what is right and what is unjust. She appeared to be surprised that a judge would allow her unusual display of conscience in a courtroom.

In that moment, Marian took a deep breath, as if she was inhaling new life. She sat taller and straighter in her chair.

"Now," I said, "let's see how we can help you." I asked a clinical intern to speak with her privately to gather needed information and make treatment recommendations to the court. Our goal would be to link Marian to housing and an integrated behavioral health treatment program where she could address her clinical needs and begin the process of healing.

Those who get the benefit of this court accept a responsibility that goes along with it. To participate is to undertake a monumental amount of personal and societal responsibility. The goal for each person is not simply recovery—that would be too narrow and even inhumane if it were defined by purely data-driven results. Instead, the court's mission aims to install a spirit of "health activation," an impulse to pursue life at its fullest. In other words, to become a leader in one's own life.

I paused and looked to Marian, who was still listening intently.

Marian nodded and smiled. She had, finally, been heard.

CHAPTER 5

Simple Dreams

Seth Staumbach stood before the bench, bright-eyed and pensive. It was years since I had seen Seth. My thoughts returned to a scene years before. It took place in a hallway on the Seminole Unit at South Florida State Hospital in Pembroke Pines. As a plaintiff's monitor I was trying to conduct a meeting with Seth's mental health technician, an assistant who generally works in a hospital or institution and works in a supporting role, giving care to people with serious mental health conditions.

The noise and commotion of the hospital hallway were overwhelming. The mental health tech was saying something about staff trying to keep Seth from swallowing the cap of a soda bottle.

In 1993, prior to my election as judge, I had been hired by Florida's Advocacy Center for Persons with Disabilities (now known as Disability Rights Florida) as the plaintiff's monitor in the federal class action known as *Sanbourne v. Chiles*.[1] (A plaintiff's monitor is responsible for overseeing the implementation of the terms and conditions of the stipulated consent decree in a federal class action on behalf of the class.)

The original lawsuit had been filed in 1989; the class of plaintiffs consisted of all residents at South Florida State Hospital and those who had resided at the state hospital up to eighteen months prior to their discharge. Plaintiffs were suing the governor of Florida, Bob Martinez; Gregory L. Coler, in his capacity as secretary of the Florida Department of Health and Rehabilitative Services; David Sofferin, in his official capacity as administrator of South Florida State Hospital; and R. J. Castellanos, in his official capacity as acting director of Division of Risk Management, State of Florida. The class action, filed in 1991, involved the care and treatment of persons with mental illness confined to South Florida State Hospital: conditions at the hospital were inhumane, physically and emotionally debilitating.

The consent decree I had been hired to monitor focused on the discharge planning process. As plaintiff's monitor, I spent my days at the state hospital meeting with class members, reviewing care plans, and attending discharge planning meetings. Each day when I arrived, the first thing I did was check to see if anyone had been added to the discharge planning list. If so, I would visit that person to introduce myself, review the person's rights under the consent decree, and begin to engage in that individual's care plan and discharge planning process. My other key duties involved following clients into the community upon their discharge from the state hospital to evaluate the quality or the lack of quality of the discharge plans and then report back to senior counsel at Southern Legal Counsel, Alice K. Nelson.

The suit sought relief from the court for civil rights violations. Allegations included the type of maltreatment and indignities shown in films such as the 1948 film *The Snake Pit* and in *Life* magazine's groundbreaking exposé on the abuse of psychiatric patients, "Bedlam 1946—Most US Mental Hospitals Are a Shame and Disgrace." This article documented the beatings and murders of more than 400,000 psychiatric patients who were confined in 180 psychiatric state hospitals throughout the United States.[2] *Sanbourne v. Chiles* contained allegations of wide-ranging abuse and neglect at the South Florida State Hospital. These allegations included "a lack of rehabilitation and complete lack of privacy and control over the most basic and routine aspects of life."[3] More specifically, plaintiffs cited group nakedness and a failure to provide personal clothing; instead, "communal clothing" was distributed by staff daily.[4] Additional allegations included that the conditions of the physical plant of the hospital were intolerable, staff abuse was rampant, and a lack of basic dental care consigned the plaintiffs to a considerable amount of unnecessary discomfort.[5] Susan Curran, a hospital surveyor who testified on behalf of the Advocacy Center for Persons with Disabilities, was quoted in the *Palm Beach Post* as saying, "We broke down and cried at what we saw."[6]

When it came to Seth, I don't know which specific conditions he experienced in the state hospital. He entered the system as an adolescent, and despite the love and support of his family, who tried to make the experience as positive as it could be, he struggled. I can only imagine what life inside the state hospital must have been like. His unit was one among many on a campus consisting of military-style barracks and minimal landscaping. Inside these residential barracks, long, winding corridors amplified noise. Seth's days, in his unit, would have been filled with the sounds of screams from other unit tenants in an unchanging landscape of gray. He never attended a typical school, went to a prom or homecoming dance, played sports, or joined a debate team. He never learned to drive.

Even with the loving support of his family, Seth experienced a kind of life that I cannot imagine.

When I joined the Advocacy Center, the parties had already been working for several years to improve conditions at the state hospital. These negotiations were in accordance with the earlier ruling of the US District Court, Southern District, Miami, to work toward resolving the problems and settling the lawsuit. The negotiations involved the court's 1991 ruling on the plaintiff's motion for summary judgment.[7] At the same time, members of the Florida legislature moved to close the state hospital, in order to limit the liability of the state for the maltreatment uncovered by the suit.[8]

The conflation of these events led the state to make significant improvements at the state hospital and to undertake efforts to move reforms toward a community-based system of care. In exchange for a consent decree between parties settled in 1993 the state pledged to infuse the state hospital catchment areas with substantial funding to enhance community-based resources for mental health.

This left two questions for class members and the community: Would legislative funding be sufficient to drive transformational change of South Florida's beleaguered mental health system? And what would happen to *Sanbourne* class members in the meantime?

On February 5, 1963, President John F. Kennedy addressed Congress in support of what would be a series of legislative measures known as the Community Mental Health Act.[9] In a special message to the Congress, President Kennedy shared his transformative vision to shift the nation away from its reliance upon an antiquated and dangerous system of state institutions and hospitals to care for and house those with mental illness.[10] At the time, nearly eight hundred thousand patients were confined in mental hospitals, six hundred thousand for mental health problems and two hundred thousand for mental retardation. These were people with disabilities who, in Kennedy's words, "have been kept out of sight and forgotten."[11] Kennedy had a special interest in ushering in a new era in mental health having had a sister, Rosemary, who had intellectual disabilities and lived in a private institution for much of her adult life.

President Kennedy spoke of a "troubled national conscience" and a moral urgency for Congress to address this public health crisis.[12] While Kennedy expressed appreciation for states' efforts to improve the conditions of state institutions, he recognized the need for the federal government to bring its resources and energies to bear on the problem. He called for all levels of government and the private sector to share in taking responsibility to improve health in the areas of mental health and mental retardation.

Citing research findings pertaining to the need to develop a new systemic approach to healthcare, Kennedy relied upon a study by the Joint Commission on Mental Illness and Health and its final report, which appeared in 1961.[13] He noted key facts illustrating the urgent need for Congress to support his proposals:

- Nearly one-fifth of the 279 state mental institutions are fire hazards; three-quarters of them were built prior to World War I.
- Nearly half of the 530,000 patients in our state mental hospitals are in institutions with over 3,000 patients, where individual care is virtually impossible.
- Many of the institutions have less than half the professional staff required—less than 1 psychiatrist for every 360 patients.
- Forty-five percent of the inmates have been hospitalized continuously for ten years or more.

The president referred to the positive research and recommendations of the commission, which pointed to a new trend in mental health care and rehabilitation: the use of new drugs and "a growing public awareness" about mental illness and community-based care.[14]

Kennedy's visionary blueprint was consistent with the recommendations of the commission, which envisioned a mental-health-care system focused on prevention that would include a broad range of treatment and restorative programmatic services such as community mental health centers, psychiatric beds, day-care respite centers, crisis services, and other community facilities to provide treatment and rehabilitative services in the "open warmth of community."[15] The president's goal was to shift patients into local mental health centers, reduce the state hospitals' population by 50 percent, and ultimately eliminate the need for most state hospitals.[16] On October 31, 1963, Kennedy signed into law the Mental Retardation and Community Mental Health Centers Construction Act, more commonly known as the Community Mental Health Act.[17] It would his last legislative action before his death.

By the 1990s, the failings of the deinstitutionalization movement were evident. The Florida legislature pledged a significant infusion of funds, about $25 million, for community-based services to support the downsizing of the state hospital. Yet for Seth and thousands of residents residing in state hospitals across the nation, the hospital that was failing them was the only home they knew.[18]

My duties as plaintiff's monitor were complex and often contentious, as my role pitted me against the State of Florida. I advocated on behalf of my clients who had been discharged from the state hospital to the community. My jurisdiction was six feeder counties across the southern half of the state. Soon after I was appointed to the position, I started to question the effectiveness of my advocacy. The more I built positive relationships with state hospital employees, the more tensions with the state seemed to intensify. On the positive side, the state legislature allocated about $20 million to the provision of community resources for mental health patients, which led to the development of Florida's first assertive community treatment teams (interdisciplinary teams of case managers and psychiatric clinical staff), a mobile crisis unit, the first consumer drop-in centers, and other community-based resources. But supportive housing and residential programming were still in short supply. Class members may have been linked to psychosocial programs, but housing options were limited and marginal. Many *Sanbourne* class members were discharged to non-therapeutic group homes and assisted-living facilities.

In time, I decided that I might be more effective in a judicial role and left my position as plaintiff's monitor to run for an open judicial seat. I was elected in 1996.

Seth had burned many bridges while a patient at the state hospital. He was constantly "redirected" by staff, meaning that they attempted to manage his behavior from inappropriate to appropriate through various therapeutic strategies. He obsessively repeated various self-injurious behaviors, so it was difficult for Seth to make advances in his rehabilitation. No one at the time could imagine that Seth would one day inspire "the Seth line," an alternative to a crisis line, staffed by trained consumers who listen to callers' concerns and provide support and advice on a peer-to-peer basis.

As I began to deal with Seth's case, I speculated that he was probably one of the last residents to be discharged from the state hospital in the 1990s. He had been institutionalized as an adolescent in the early to mid-seventies, when his intellectual disabilities and behavioral disorders became severe enough to require constant supervision. Hospital staff had significant concerns regarding his capacity for self-harm. His deep behavioral problems led to many staffing issues, as frustration on his unit ran high.

Yet here he was in court, a middle-aged man now, looking much more mature and different then I remembered him.

"Judge Ginger," Seth called out happily, "it's good to see you!" Seth was always so excited to come to court: here, he had conversations with people, and he was asked about his life. It was a stark difference from what he experienced in the hospital. Yet after a moment, his jubilant smile faded. Perhaps thinking he had said too much or was too enthusiastic, his face now reflected anxiety as he began to stammer, "I'm sorry—I'm sorry," repeating this in an anxious, high tone.

"It's OK, Seth," I replied. "I'm happy to see you, too."

Standing next to him, looking more like a protective big brother than a mental health advocate, was Jack Kuhn, his former case manager at the Henderson Behavioral Health Center. Today, Jack would serve as Seth's housing coach and residential administrator.

Jack was one of my mentors when I began my position as plaintiff's monitor with the Advocacy Center. He was the first community case manager I met at the state hospital. Our initial conversation back then, which occurred as we stood next to a large round garbage can in the hospital courtyard, led to years of friendship.

Jack came from a large family in Nashville, Tennessee. He was smart and could have chosen any profession, but he wanted to be a social worker. It was a vocation that, he said, "my father did not appreciate or support."

Jack retired from Henderson after the death of his father, a Nashville businessman, who profited from the sale of his family's Big K chain of discount stores to Sam Walton of Walmart.[19] Turning to philanthropy, Jack fulfilled his lifelong dream when he launched Simple Dreams, a foundation whose mission was to provide housing for mental health consumers.

At the time, Jack was an intensive community case manager, and I was new to the job of plaintiff's monitor. There were so many facets to this role, but the first order of business for me was to understand the fundamentals of discharge planning from a community level. Jack generously offered to allow me to shadow him during community visits. This experience was profoundly important because Jack taught me the essential principles of person-centered psychiatric rehabilitation based on data-driven research from Boston University's Center for Psychiatric Rehabilitation. These principles were being applied at South Florida State Hospital and in the community to foster a person-centered and psychosocial culture across Broward County's system of mental health care.[20] Working with Jack, I learned how important it is to develop positive relationships with community-based case managers and hospital-based discharge planners when collaborating and negotiating for scarce resources on behalf of your clients, people like Seth, who wanted to experience his "simple dream" of residing in the warmth of the community.

"Judge, I wanted to let you know that Seth is doing very well," Jack said.

Jack knew Seth and his parents, Chuck and Gayle Staumbach, a delightful couple who have been mental health advocates in Broward County since the mid-1970s, when Seth had been committed to South Florida State Hospital as a teenager. Warm and eager to support other families, the Staumbachs worked closely with the Mental Health Association of Southeast Florida. A local Broward affiliate of Mental Health America, the Mental Health Association of Southeast Florida was chartered in 1957 and is still dedicated to promoting mental health through education, prevention, research, and advocacy.

I now learned the reason for Seth's appearance in my courtroom. Apparently, he had been arrested for stealing some snacks from a local convenience store, an incident that, Jack stated, "he was already on top of."

"I want you to know what steps Seth and I have taken to ensure that something like this does not happen again," Jack said.

In a conventional criminal court setting, I would not permit an attorney or any person to discuss the facts of a case. As the presiding judge, I advise defendants not to comment about their cases. This advice is meant to protect their constitutional right to remain silent and to prevent them from saying anything that could be used against them, should their case proceed to trial. Because I knew that there was no reasonable likelihood that Seth's case would proceed to trial, I allowed Jack's comments. Further, I recognized that Jack was speaking about psychiatric rehabilitative strategies, which Seth had already agreed to. I agreed that sharing these steps with the court would be therapeutic for Seth and put him more at ease with court process.

"Go on, Mr. Kuhn," I said, now intrigued about what kind of creative steps Jack had implemented to keep Seth safe to and prevent further behaviors that could get Seth arrested again.

"Well, Judge," Jack began, "I realize that although Seth spent many years at the hospital, he likes people and enjoys being independent." He spoke like a college professor delivering a lecture to a class of social work students. He continued: "Seth has opened a small bank account, and I am working with him to establish a weekly budget. Seth receives a certain amount of money each month, and this experience has taught him how much money he has allocated for food and snacks. In fact, we took a walk to the community store where this situation occurred to meet with the manager."

Jack continued, with a giant grin on his face, knowing full well that I would be impressed with the new and improved case management plan that had already been implemented. "Seth and I had a meeting with the general manager and we discussed Seth's goals to become more independent in the community. I gave the store manager my card and let him know that Seth is only permitted to come to the store with a shopping buddy who will ensure he has the correct amount of money with him."

"That sounds like a sensible and responsible plan," I said.

The state attorney, who had been listening silently, chimed in. "Judge, I agree with you that Mr. Kuhn sounds like he is overseeing his client very well, but I suggest we follow Mr. Staumbach in the court, to ensure he is following his case management plan." This meant that the court would monitor Seth through a series of review hearings in order to monitor his case management plan and his compliance to treatment and its effectiveness, to troubleshoot problems proactively, and to oversee the accountability of his community-based treatment provider.

Janis agreed that given Seth's history of behavioral challenges it would be helpful for him to be followed by the court. "It would bolster his behavioral plan in the community and give him more opportunity to socialize and be around people," she said.

Janis had spoken with Jack prior to the hearing and was advised that Seth was not interested in attending a day treatment program focused on mental health. Janis did not want Seth to become isolated. "He needs to connect with people," she said.

Seth agreed. "I would like to stay in the court—and my parents wanted me to say hello because they could not come with me today." Seth's participation in the mental health court was voluntary, and he was stating his desire to continue his participation.

I smiled at him, accepting the greeting Seth had relayed to me. "You know, Seth," I said, "in a few months the court is holding its fifth anniversary celebration and 'Triumph Awards' luncheon. I would love to have you as one of our honorees."

Attorney General Janet Reno would be our special guest. I wasn't sure Seth knew who Janet Reno was, but it was a great honor to have her there. During her time as US attorney general Reno dispatched several high-ranking members of her office to observe the Broward County Mental Health Court. The following year, Attorney General Reno identified Broward's court as an emerging best practice.[21] As a former Miami-Dade County state attorney, Janet Reno pioneered the first drug court in 1989.[22] She was a great advocate of court innovation and problem-solving treatment courts.

Janet Reno took office as Miami-Dade County state attorney in 1978. While speaking to an audience of drug court professionals, nearly a decade after Miami launched America's first drug court, Reno described how she watched as the criminal justice system in Miami-Dade County became "swamped" by cases involving people being arrested for possessing "small amounts" of drugs and then larger amounts of drugs, where first-time offenders entered a revolving door of arrests due to drug addiction.[23] She realized that alternatives to incarceration must include drug treatment, but saw a system that offered no interventions. On March 24, 1998, at a conference in Washington, DC, Reno stated, "When I first took office, in 1978, people did not believe in treatment. And I could not understand why. But I quickly learned that unless we made treatment an effective alternative to incarceration, we were never going to build our way out of the problem."[24]

At the end of the hearing, I caught Jack's eye and smiled. I thought back to the horrible living conditions on the Seminole Unit at the state hospital where I first met Janis and Jack, where many of the patients, like Seth, had lived at the hospital for decades.

Seeing Seth after so many years, I wonder how Aaron Wynn's life would have changed had he received any reasonable level of mental health care and services after his tragic motorcycle accident. Aaron Wynn is now living in a private hospital for people with traumatic brain injury in central Florida. The jury's award of $18 million for violation of Aaron's civil rights, based upon negligent care and maltreatment at a Florida forensic hospital, was sufficient to provide for his rehabilitation and care.[25] Having a safe and decent place to live in the community that we call home seems like such a simple dream—one that many of us take for granted.

CHAPTER 6

I Once Was Lost

The Broward County Mental Health Court never called into question the life experience or history of a person who "claimed to be homeless." That was the case until we heard Beatrice St. Fleur's story that brought this issue to light. For the first time, the court heard the story of a person who was truly—and in every way—"lost." The mystery surrounding Ms. St. Fleur's identity and where she was from taught us always to inquire about life experiences. Ms. St. Fleur was from the Bahamas, but no one knew how she had gotten to Florida or why she was in Broward County.

I am shocked at how many of the people referred to mental health court who are classified as homeless are actually *missing*. This means that for some unknown reason they walked, ran, or wandered away from their lives, which might have included a job, a family, a home, and they had chosen an anonymous and unattached life instead.

The difference between being chronically homeless and being missing is significant for many reasons. For one thing, the whereabouts of the chronically homeless are not necessarily unknown, whereas a missing person literally "disappears" from their previous life. And while homelessness is, at times, congruent with "missing," it is important to remember that not all who suffer from homelessness are missing, and those who are missing are not necessarily homeless. The difference lies in the connection one maintains with one's family, friends, and community. When someone suddenly disappears, those ties are severed, as if the person had suddenly been erased.

This is why, in the case of a missing person, it is impossible to describe the emotional impact of reuniting a family. As I dial the number of a client's father or mother and wait for the phone to be answered, the courtroom invariably goes quiet. We all wait in suspense as I do my best to remain matter of fact, in the event the call does not go through. More than likely, however, a family member answers.

"Hello," I say, "my name is Judge Ginger Lerner-Wren." I explain to the party on the other line where I am calling from and ask them if they know the subject of the call. It is both heartbreaking and exhilarating to hear cries of relief when they realize that the call is authentic and their loved one who had inexplicably disappeared is alive and safe.

When Beatrice St. Fleur, a middle-aged Bahamian woman, was escorted into the mental health court, her distressed state and a language barrier meant that I was initially unable to tell what exactly had, weeks before, brought her to Florida from the Bahamas. According to her paperwork, she had been arrested for allegedly failing to pay a $22 cab fare, but aside from that, I could glean little to nothing about her life other than something had gone terribly wrong.

Beatrice became, in my mind, another one of those individuals who had gone missing from their own lives. Sometimes this is understandable, since in a traditional courtroom setting defendants aren't permitted to tell the stories of their own lives. In a traditional court, it is the attorney who addresses the court, not the defendant or the subject of the hearing. The only time a litigant may be permitted to talk about his or her personal histories may be at various legal phases of the court process, such as a sentencing hearing or when a court must make rulings concerning matters of mental competency to stand trial and mental capacity. Otherwise, defendants are mute observers to the court proceedings resulting from their actions and lives.

In a problem-solving mental health court, this is not at all the case—especially not in the Broward County Mental Health Court, which applies a therapeutic justice approach that encourages clients to tell their personal stories. When they talk about their life experiences, court participants are given a voice and the court process is humanized.

Beatrice St. Fleur sat with her head down, handcuffed to a chair in the jury box. Her light blue jail jumpsuit acted like camouflage, blending into the scene of the courtroom. Aisha McDonald, the criminal justice liaison for Chrysalis Behavioral Health Center, a local Behavioral Health Center that is committed to serving persons in the criminal justice system, began speaking with her. Aisha's family is Jamaican. She not only provides cultural context for the court but also has the unique ability to bridge cultural differences when explaining the court's mission. South Florida is very culturally diverse, with large Caribbean and Haitian populations. According to 2011 data, Broward County was the third most ethnically and racially diverse county in Florida.[1] In 2015, its population was 40.4 percent white, 26.9 percent African American, and 27 percent Hispanic, and it had the largest concentration of Caribbean immigrants in the United States.[2] So it has been wonderful to have Aisha's help.

"Judge," Aisha said with alarm, "I think you should speak to Ms. St. Fleur. She keeps repeating that she needs to get back to her children, but she does not know where they are."

Beatrice responded, but I was unable to understand her. The conversation ran in circles. After several rounds of trying to gather basic information, such as where she was from and who was taking care of her children, Beatrice said that she was a Bahamian lawyer and had to return home immediately to find her children. Unfortunately, she couldn't tell us where "home" was.

I stopped asking Beatrice questions, for both Janis and Aisha pointed out that she was becoming agitated. I asked Digna, the court clerk, for an emergency transportation order to get Beatrice to Henderson Behavioral Health Center's Crisis Stabilization Unit. In the meantime, I thought about other court participants, like Kathryn and Lilly, who had been traumatized by forced separation from their children.

Trauma had contributed to Kathryn's decision to abandon the home she had worked so hard to acquire and to turn to the streets. Lilly's trauma, on the other hand, kept her returning to her home despite a judge's order awarding custody of the children to her ex-husband and a restraining order to keep her from returning to her former residence. If we could learn a little bit more about Beatrice St. Fleur, I was confident that we could help her find a family member or someone who knew her well enough to help us get her back home.

The question of who is truly homeless and who is missing is more than a nuance. We have learned from experience that people go missing for various reasons and in various circumstances, including untreated mental illness. Sometimes families file a missing person's report, but more often than not, no report is filed. It must be a strange thing to discover that someone who is an integral part of your life has simply vanished: there one moment, gone the next. In dysfunctional families it is quite possible that no one will file a missing person alert.

When I speak to family members, they often express frustration relating to their loved one's inability to follow their prescribed treatment plan. In many cases, substance abuse is involved, as individuals turn to self-medication, which aggravates existing tensions and anxieties about their deteriorating health and the possibility of incarceration. According to recent data from the National Institute of Mental Health, "20.2 million adults in the US had a substance use disorder and 7.9 million had both a substance use disorder and another mental illness. More than half of the people with both a substance use disorder and another mental illness were men (4.1 million)."[3] As they sink further into oblivion due to whatever substance they have chosen—alcohol or drugs—the person they once were also slips away. The ties that keep families together are

stretched as a loved one falls into addiction, while the family strug-
gles to support their loved one in the hopes of promoting recovery
and preventing further justice involvement and the revolving door
of incarceration.[4]

Many family members report feelings of fatigue due to unend-
ing stress and the pressures of attempting to care for other family
members and to maintain their jobs while trying to manage their
son or daughter's mental health problems. In many cases, it is simply too much.

Each situation is unique and entails a high level of coordination,
particularly if the family lives out of state. One reason for the complexity is my requirement that individuals who are subject to reunification with their families must be escorted back home. This is
for safety purposes and to ensure integrity of the reunification plan.
For individuals who live outside Florida, this means relatives or a
designated surrogate must come to the courtroom or jail to pick
the person up and accompany them home where they can begin
the process of rebuilding and rehabilitation. According to Mental
Health America, access to mental health care varies from state to
state, and one out of five (20.1 percent) adults with a mental illness
report they are unable to get treatment at all.[5] Mental health court
staff provide families with the names of local mental health centers and resources to assist in coordination of care upon their return
home and to gain the support of family members and the community to build resilience and promote recovery.[6]

Over the past two decades, I have witnessed how the internet has
advanced the court's ability to reunite people with their families.
Now, through online research, we can take the fragments of information we receive from people whose mental capacity is diminished because of illness and separate fact from delusion. People who
go missing can be more easily found—online traces of their lives
facilitate their return to their existence in the real world.

Years ago, a young man in his twenties was diagnosed with
schizophrenia and was referred to the mental health court for erratic
behavior in a public place. He identified himself as a graduate student in a school of business in Connecticut. Prior to the existence

of the internet, this shred of information would have taken several months to track down and verify, but an online search verified his testimony within seconds. Further review of the school's website confirmed the name of the master's program. When I called his father in Connecticut to tell him that I had his son in the courtroom, he confirmed that his son was a graduate student and that he did not know his son had been arrested.

His father stated that he was aware of his son's erratic behavior but did not recognize it as mental illness. He assumed that his son had been out of contact with him due to the demands of the graduate program. He had no idea that his son was in Florida or that he would have any reason to be involved with a court of any variety.

The mystery surrounding Beatrice St. Fleur deepened. Her public defender reported that she had contacted the jail to determine whether her client had any identification or passport in her possession when she was arrested. There was none. The property that was inventoried upon Ms. St. Fleur's arrest included a purse, wallet, and three one-dollar bills. There was no way to confirm where she lived in the Bahamas or whether her assertion to the court about being an attorney was true.

I remembered that I knew an attorney who had recently appeared in my regular criminal division who was a professor in Caribbean law and practiced immigration law. I called his office and asked if he could stop by the courtroom. Within the next few days, he came by and I explained the vexing problem we were having with Beatrice. Did he know of a way to check if she was an attorney in the Bahamas and whether there was a family law case pending? The attorney generously agreed to assist and went to the hospital to visit her.

It did not take long before we learned that Beatrice was a victim of domestic violence. She told the attorney, "My husband threatened to kill me if I did not give him custody of our three children." She took the threat seriously and felt she had no choice but to leave the household, and the island.

The attorney decided to go through the Bahamian consulate and review Beatrice's status. He confirmed that she was a Bahamian citizen and an attorney. The consulate agreed to replace her passport, and the attorney worked to intervene on her behalf in the family courts.

When I heard this, I was taken aback. I thanked him, but explained that it was not my intention that he should represent Beatrice on a pro bono basis. I had no idea that she was a victim of domestic violence. Apparently, she was so distraught that she fled with nothing but the clothes on her back. He indicated that he was pleased to help and wanted to assist her with reuniting with her children and to represent her on the petit theft case (petit theft is a misdemeanor charge in which a person has stolen property that is valued at under $300 without the intent of returning it).

I was overcome with gratitude.

After several weeks in the hospital, Beatrice returned to court for a follow-up hearing upon her release from the hospital. She was feeling much better and explained that when her husband threatened to kill her, she was already on the brink of an emotional breakdown.

As an attorney, she said she had filed a petition for divorce and custody of the children. From a cultural perspective, she stated that her estranged husband was angry and humiliated that she was planning to disclose the history of domestic violence to the court. She would disgrace his name if she did that, and that was the moment when the threats began.

"That was when he commenced an intensive campaign of psychological and emotional abuse," she said. He warned her that no one would believe her claims of domestic violence and her family would disown her. As the emotional abuse intensified, Beatrice's mental health declined.

Soon, the anxiety was unmanageable. "I could not take anymore," she said. She felt unsafe and alone.

She had no memory about her decision to leave her home, her family, and everything she knew and cared about. As victims of abuse and trauma commonly report, her mind stopped recording accessible memory and she turned to a flight-or-fight response. "I was in a panic when I purchased a one-way ticket, and I don't know why I chose Fort Lauderdale," she said.

"Do you feel safe enough to return?" I asked.

"While I was at the hospital I made plans to live with family on the other side of the island, and the children are already with them. It seems that the threats about seeking custody of the children were not authentic but intended to instill fear and intimidation. When I called my family, they did not know what had happened to me. They feared the worse."

I heard the unspoken words: "I had gone missing. I had been erased and no one was sure that I would ever return."

As I watched the petite woman prepare to return to her home and family, I imagine that Beatrice's mental health might have deteriorated in jail if the Broward County Mental Health Court hadn't intervened. She might have ended up on the streets or trapped in the criminal justice system as issues of mental competency would more than likely need to be determined by the judge. All over a $22 cab fare. Thankfully, she was diverted from the jail and received psychiatric treatment in a setting where she could feel safe.

Not all cases end so well. I soon learned that the young business school student from Connecticut had another criminal case pending in Palm Beach County from the assistant state attorney. No matter what we in the mental health court did, we could not reunite him with his family because of his other criminal case.

I called his father from the phone on my bench at his next status hearing and canceled any plan for reunification. I informed him that the criminal case pending in Palm Beach County was a felony and that the judge had revoked his bond, based upon his new arrest. I told him that the only thing I could do was to release him on the Broward case, which would free him to return to Palm Beach County to face the more serious charge. His public defender would do her best to advocate for him through the Palm Beach Public Defender's Office. It was an incredibly painful conversation.

His father was distraught. He interrupted my words of consolation to protest that his son was just fine and not suffering from a mental illness. "Judge, we are a Jamaican family, and we really don't discuss mental health, and I am not familiar with these things." He nearly began to cry.

"Judge, there is a great deal of shame surrounding mental illness in the Jamaican culture," his defense attorney said.[7]

There was nothing I could do but state the facts as they were. He thanked me for my help and for taking the time to call him.

"At least, Judge, we know where our son is. He is not missing," he said.

CHAPTER 7

Therapeutic Justice Goes Mainstream

In 2005, eight years after the Broward County Mental Health Court's founding, the principles and goals of therapeutic jurisprudence had become more than a judicial philosophy applied in the court. Over time, this restorative and problem-solving approach had become a core element of my judicial role in my regular criminal division, which is adversarial and process driven. It was clear, when I encountered Michael Evans sitting in the courtroom between dockets, that therapeutic jurisprudence is a universal practice in the law and not limited to problem-solving courts such as the mental health court.

I observed Mr. Evans as he sat in the middle row of an otherwise nearly empty courtroom; clearly he was extremely fearful, and I could not help but be concerned. I watched as he quietly gasped for air in a failed attempt to hold back tears. I could not tell which court division he was scheduled to appear in. He was either a late comer to the mental health court or an early arrival for the regular criminal division. In either case, it was evident that he required assistance.

In regular court divisions, where the courtrooms operate in a more formal manner, I would expect a court deputy to check on the welfare of this person, if he or she had detected a problem. And if there was indeed a problem, I believe that a court deputy would bring it to the judge's attention. More than likely, however, I expect that the person would probably tell the deputy that everything was fine so as not to draw attention to himself or disrupt the proceedings. As noted by David B. Wexler, the cofounder of therapeutic jurisprudence, judges and other members of the legal system often have been aware of the impact of the legal system on individual cases—for example, a judge will offer a witness who is overcome with emotion a brief recess; or a defendant will be permitted to settle a case to avoid the undue stress of the court process. But with the justice innovation of therapeutic jurisprudence came a "general theory" of the impact of the legal process upon a court participant's well-being and its implications for achieving restorative outcomes.[1]

Since this was a therapeutic and person-centered courtroom, and the session had not begun, I felt compelled to check on him myself. I sat down next to him while my court deputy kept watch.

"Sir, can we talk?" I asked. I did not wait for a response but immediately asked another question: "What's wrong. Can I help you?"

"I just lost my job and our home is about to go into foreclosure," he cried. "I have tried everything. I am fearful for my family." He paused and gulped before he said, almost in a whisper, "I feel like giving up."

I sat in silence as Mr. Evans began to sob. It was clear to me that in this state he did not have the emotional capacity to participate in a court hearing and needed a mental health professional. I told him that I would be right back and returned to the bench.

I asked Digna, my court clerk, to look up Mr. Evans's case on the docket. She discovered that he was not in the mental health court. He had been charged with petit theft and assigned to my regular criminal division.

As presiding judge I had several options. I could provide him information on where to go for mental health services and reschedule his court date for another day. Yet, given his deep level of emotional distress and his comment that he felt like giving up, I did not think that leaving the situation in its current state was appropriate.

With a heightened sense of alarm, I decided to call Henderson Behavioral Health Center's mobile crisis team. There have been many occasions when I needed to call the mobile crisis team to the courtroom. This is particularly true when an individual would come to court alone, in obvious distress and crisis, and I would have no legal authority to transport him or her to a psychiatric hospital or receiving facility for evaluation. Like Michael Evans, who sat on the court bench in tears, I could have no idea of the depth of his despair or whether he was contemplating harming himself. And I learned many years ago that these situations must be taken very seriously. I reflected on an earlier case when a mental health court defendant tried to see me and was turned away.

Harold Simmons was chronically homeless. When he showed up unexpectedly in the middle of jury selection for my criminal division, I did not know who he was. As he tried to enter the courtroom, he was immediately intercepted by the court deputy, who ushered him into the hallway so as not to disrupt the trial.

After a few minutes, the deputy returned to the courtroom. When court recessed, I inquired about the person who had walked in. "Judge, his name is Harold Simmons. He was in your mental health court several years ago and asked if he could speak with you. I explained that you were in trial and would be unable to speak to him."

I nodded and speculated that it was probably a minor matter and refocused my attention on the trial.

Within a matter of weeks, alarming news about the emerging local opioid crisis broke across the state.[2] More than a decade later, the opioid crisis in America and the state of Florida has become a national public health crisis. In November 2016, Governor Rick Scott declared a state of emergency in order to draw down federal funds and raise the alarm in Florida that the opioid crisis had reached a critical level. According to *NBC News*, "The Governor of Florida officially declared the opioid epidemic a public health emergency—some four years after it began cutting a deadly swath through the Sunshine State."[3] Governor Scott's declaration has allowed the state to tap more than $54 million in US Department of Health funds.

One morning about a week after the governor's declaration, the conversation in the mental health court focused on the urgent need for a strategic public health response and additional detox and drug treatment resources in the community to combat the crisis.

"That is so true, Judge!" exclaimed a woman named Sylvia, who was sitting in a wheelchair next to the jury box. In her mid-fifties, Sylvia was homeless and had been arrested for trespassing. In an obvious need to share her loss, she continued, "Just last week, my friend Harold Simmons was found dead on a bus bench. He died from a drug overdose."

The name Simmons triggered a memory. I thought of the man who had wanted to speak to me a week before. I wondered, with dread, if that had been him. A sinking feeling crept from my stomach to my chest: *That must have been him.* I sat in shock. *What if I had stopped the proceedings to speak to him? Or, simply asked him to wait in the courtroom until I could speak to him?*

I wondered whether this tragedy could have been avoided.

When the session concluded, I met with my court deputies. I instructed them to please speak to anyone coming to the courtroom who wanted to speak with me and to ask them the purpose of their visit. It wouldn't matter whether they had a case pending before the court. The deputies would always make an inquiry as to whether a person required assistance. Then, he or she would determine how to respond.

As I explained this new policy, the reason why it was needed hung heavily in the room. Speaking directly but softly, I realized that I was talking about the possibility that a person may need immediate attention. It was a painful and transformative moment.

It has been eight years since the court began, and in this moment, I realized that Howard Finkelstein's vision to create a court of refuge had come to fruition in a way we had not foreseen.

Since that time, an estimated 150 people have come to the courtroom in need of services or in the middle of a mental health crisis. If necessary, I take a break from proceedings to address their problems and to avoid another situation like that of Harold Simmons. If that is not possible, I ask JoAnne Capiello, my judicial assistant, to see whether Aisha McDonald from Chrysalis Behavioral Health Center was in the building and request that she come to assist the person.

If I suspect that crisis services are necessary, I call Henderson's mobile crisis team to the courtroom. For this option, however, the person must be willing to wait—and often negotiation is necessary to persuade the person to stay until the team arrives. We have learned that people are more apt to wait when I personally invite them to observe the activities of the court.

The clinicians who make up Henderson's mobile crisis team are specially trained in techniques to de-escalate crises; their clinical objective is to assess and manage the crisis. Their understated dress—casual clothes such as jeans, T-shirts, and sneakers—matches their mild manners when they interact with the public, law enforcement, or anyone in the Broward County Mental Health Court. They are the ultimate determiners of who requires emergency mental health attention. After screening and consultation, they may recommend that the person seek mental health care on an outpatient basis.

The team goes anywhere within the county. In fact, one weekend as I was getting my hair done at a local hair salon, I heard yelling emanating from the rear of the salon. As my attention turned to see what was happening, I observed an elderly woman behaving erratically. I walked over to get a closer look, and the woman appeared not to be making sense. I asked the salon manager not to call the police but to allow me to call the mobile crisis team.

Since the manager knew about my work in the court, she appreciated my assistance and allowed me to make the call. Fortunately, they were not far away and arrived within minutes.

When the team entered the salon, my head was covered with layers of tin foil. When the team members saw me, they smiled and proceeded to speak to the woman in distress.

After a few minutes, they helped the woman exit the salon and confirmed that she was going to the hospital for evaluation. The experience provided years of comic relief, as I joked that team members were under oath not to publicly talk about the judge's hair.

As I returned to considering Michael Evans, I considered how to suggest to him that I thought the mobile crisis team needed to be called. I hoped he would agree and was concerned as to whether Mr. Evans would agree to wait for the team to arrive. Broward County has only one mobile crisis team to serve an estimated population of 1.8 million people, a situation that I hope will improve soon. In fact, Henderson Behavioral Health Center was recently awarded a $21.9 million grant by the Florida Department of Children and Families to establish a countywide centralized receiving system designed to expand access to mental health and crisis services so people like Harold Simmons and Michael Evans won't ever be forced to wait outside closed doors.[4]

I calmly took a seat next to Mr. Evans and handed him some tissues. "Mr. Evans, I'm sorry you have been going through such a difficult time. I think it would be a good idea for me to call the Henderson crisis team, so that you can get some help now. I would greatly appreciate you waiting for the Henderson team to arrive. I think it would be helpful if you have the chance to explain to them how you are feeling."

I let Mr. Evans know that they usually arrive within thirty minutes, but it could take longer. The estimate, I hoped, was conservative. I told him that I would call to confirm the team's timeline. I asked him if this was acceptable. I could see that he was thinking it over, the details of time versus the trouble of staying here with no answers for at least another half hour, another eternity, of anxiety and worry. At this point, I got the sense that given the weight of his distress, time was of little consequence. As I spoke quietly on the line with the Henderson crisis team, I watched Evan's face. His expression voiced concern, but he waited until I confirmed the team would be there in less than fifteen minutes. Then, he told me quietly that it was.

I returned to the bench and called Henderson.

When problem-solving courts emerged in 1989, they brought the tenets of therapeutic jurisprudence with them, even though it was not a new concept. For many years, the law professors David B. Wexler and Bruce J. Winick, pioneers in the law reform movement of therapeutic jurisprudence, had long envisioned the expansion of therapeutic justice to traditional courts of general jurisdiction. This was a goal I shared with them, especially as society becomes more complex and the provision of mental health and substance abuse treatment services cannot keep up.

One day, as I listened to the assistant state attorney in my regular criminal division convey a plea offer to a young woman at her sentencing hearing, I wondered, *What exactly is the difference between the mental health court and my regular criminal division?* Most times I find myself taking a therapeutic approach to my role as judge in both courts.

The defendant, Linda Withers, in her mid-thirties, was employed as a highly successful executive for an international marketing firm. I listened as the prosecutor pronounced the conditions of the sentence that included thirty days in jail. This was Ms. Withers's second driving-under-the-influence offense within the past five years. As I reviewed the arrest affidavit and her Florida driver's license record, something did not sit right with me.

Ms. Withers had a successful career and was well educated. More important, she had no other criminal history. Furthermore, other than the DUI charges, her driving record was clean. I called the attorneys to the bench for a sidebar conference to discuss the plea offer in a more limited setting.

The defense attorney and prosecutor walked around to the side of the witness stand as I stepped down from the bench to consult with them. I explained to them that my work in the mental health court led me to think that Ms. Withers may need a psychosocial evaluation to determine whether she is suffering from unresolved trauma and in need of a therapeutic approach to her case. I was concerned about the recent driving-under-the-influence arrests and asked whether she needed more intensive mental health and alcohol treatment interventions. I added that, from a behavioral health perspective, if she did not receive the comprehensive care she obviously needed, there could be a greater potential for her to re-offend.

I reviewed basic research findings from the ACE study and the consequences of violence and trauma.[5] I suggested that Ms. Withers be screened and evaluated by Carolyn Gallichio of Advocate Counseling to act as an expert and offer treatment recommendations to the court. Ms. Gallichio was a specialist in trauma-related care and an approved school provider of programs to combat driving under the influence of alcohol.

Both parties in the case, the state attorney's office and Ms. Withers's defense attorney, welcomed the court's recommendation, and the case was reset—rescheduled for a new date—to allow a pre-sentencing evaluation.

Within ten days, Ms. Withers's case was re-called. Ms. Gallichio appeared along with Ms. Withers, her counsel, and the prosecution. Ms. Gallichio was sworn in to provide testimony under oath by the court deputy, and the hearing began. She had prepared a fourteen-page psychosocial report for the court. As I began to review the evaluation, Ms. Gallichio stated, "Judge, I want to let you know that your instincts were correct. Ms. Withers and I spent several sessions together. You will note as you review the report that there are 'events' that were disclosed that Ms. Withers has not had the opportunity to address from a psycho-therapeutic level. Ms. Withers has agreed to a long-term treatment plan and she is highly motivated to engage in this process."

Although my instincts may have been correct, I was not prepared for the disturbing facts in Ms. Withers's background contained in the report. It was evident to me as I read the report to myself that Ms. Withers had suffered serious neglect and physical abuse as a child. The youngest of three children, the report revealed that her mother was a victim of domestic violence. Her mother divorced Ms. Withers's father when Linda was ten years old, then remarried a man with a severe alcohol problem. Her mother did her best to shield the children from harm and to promote their education. However, Ms. Withers reported that at the age of fourteen she was molested by a coworker of her stepfather's when her mother was away visiting relatives. Per the report, Ms. Withers had never told her mother about the incident or emotionally addressed the history of domestic violence in her family.

Once I finished reading the report, I looked up at the parties and realized the importance of taking a therapeutic approach in my regular criminal division. How could I offer a therapeutic approach in one division and not the other?

"Ms. Withers," I said, "I know it took a great deal of courage for you to go through this evaluation process."

"Thank you, Judge. It was the first time I had ever had the opportunity to reflect on my childhood and adolescence. It was surprising how somehow in my life, I just buried these awful experiences like they never happened. I suppose the time is right, as Carolyn explained to me, to heal the wounds I have been carrying around for so many years." She paused, as if to take a deep breath, then added, "I believe I'm ready."

As the conversation shifted to the sentencing recommendation, Ms. Gallichio said, "Judge, in light of the traumatic history revealed in the report, it is my suggestion to the court that an alternative to incarceration be considered. I suggest a therapeutic, trauma-informed residential program. I believe that a jail sentence will be re-traumatizing and could worsen Ms. Withers's condition. I do not believe this is in the best interests of public safety to the community or the defendant. I also believe, based on my evaluation, that Ms. Withers should be referred to a psychiatrist for further psychiatric evaluation. I suspect her condition may require medication management."

"Thank you, Ms. Gallichio," I replied. "I would ask the state attorney and defense counsel to renegotiate the plea offer and sentence in this case to identify a residential rehabilitation program, as an alternative to incarceration, and take a trauma-informed approach to Ms. Withers's case in order for her to face her pain and fears, which have been buried for so many years."

In 1998, the National Association of State Mental Health Program Directors adopted a policy statement about the lived experience of trauma.[6] The statement said in part, "It should be a matter of best practice to ask persons who enter mental health systems, at an appropriate time, if they are experiencing or have experienced trauma in their lives."[7] According to the Substance Abuse and Mental Health Services Administration, "Trauma results from an event, series of events, or set of circumstances that is experienced by an individual as physically or emotionally harmful or threatening and that has lasting adverse effects on the individual's functioning, and physical, social, emotional, or spiritual well-being."[8]

My experience in the mental health court, together with the data on the high prevalence of trauma in the criminal justice system, made me realize that it was imperative to offer a trauma-informed approach in my regular criminal division, particularly at critical points such as plea negotiations and sentencing hearings. For example, the research demonstrates that an estimated 85 percent of incarcerated women have experienced sexual or physical abuse as a child or adolescent.[9] Further, surveys showed that large percentages of men and women participating in jail diversion programs reported having experienced a significant traumatic event prior to their incarceration.[10]

Individuals who have experienced trauma are at an elevated risk for substance abuse disorders, including abuse and dependence; mental health problems (for example, depression and anxiety symptoms or disorders, impairment in relational-social and other major life areas, other distressing symptoms, and suicide).[11] According to the Substance Abuse and Mental Health Service Administration, "Trauma-informed criminal justice responses can help to avoid re-traumatizing individuals. This increases safety for all, decreases the chance of an individual returning to criminal behavior, and supports the recovery of justice-involved women and men with serious mental illness."[12] Having the flexibility in my regular criminal division to give voice to defendants and apply therapeutic jurisprudence principles (similar to the mental health court) enables Linda Withers and other defendants the equal opportunity to experience the sentencing phase of a case from a restorative perspective.

Both parties agreed to renegotiate the plea.

"Judge," Ms. Withers said, wiping away tears, "I want to thank you for referring me to Carolyn and for helping me understand the secrets I have been too ashamed and afraid to confront. All my life I have lived in terror. If this driving-under-the-influence charge is what it took to help me, then I am grateful."

"You need to know, you are not alone, given all you have achieved in your life, despite what you have endured," I said.

As the hearing concluded, the Court Deputy called the next case on the docket. Michael Evans approached the bench. It took several minutes before I realized he was the defendant who had required the services of the Henderson Behavioral Health Center's mobile crisis team.

"Mr. Evans!" I greeted him. "I didn't recognize you. How are you?" I asked.

"Judge, I am so much better. I spent time with the therapists, and they are treating my depression. I am in therapy and I am feeling more optimistic about the future. I have a new part-time job and hope to become full-time within the next few months. Thank you for caring. . . . I don't know what would have happened if I had not gotten help soon."

I asked him what he would like to do with his case. He had been charged with allegedly stealing several plastic electrical-outlet covers from a local hardware store. He responded that he would like to enter a plea of no contest and to take responsibility for what he did.

"I will never forget this incident," he said. "I had no idea how far down I sunk, Your Honor. I felt as if I was drowning."

"I understand, Mr. Evans," I said and then called the next case.

CHAPTER 8

Brothers and Sisters

It is estimated that that at least 8.4 million Americans provide care to an adult who suffers from an emotional or mental illness.[1] As stated by the Sibling Leadership Network, siblings often become the next generation of caregivers with very little advance notice or training.[2] For many aging caretakers of their adult children, the thought about what will happen to their adult child as they themselves age and then die is too uncomfortable to consider and is often avoided.[3] Many parents "hope" that siblings will care for their mentally ill brother or sister, but without prior planning and clarification of roles or legal documentation, often siblings assume the caregiving role without needed information and without an opportunity to exercise choice.[4] Sibling caregivers are called the "club sandwich generation," as they are multitasking caregiving roles for their older parents, their own family, and their brother or sister."[5] When sibling caregivers appear in court on behalf of their brothers or sisters, I am cognizant of these pressures and do everything I can to try to ease their burden.

According to research, these competing responsibilities are often physically, emotionally, and financially challenging and can cause significant distress.[6] Caregivers for family members with mental illness provide on average thirty-two hours a week to caring for their loved ones, and about half (48 percent) report that their loved one is financially dependent on them.[7] As the need for sibling care-taking continues to grow, the unique needs and experiences of these caregivers need to be better understood. Particularly, where the research indicates that most aging parents have not engaged siblings in planning for transition into the care-taking role and do not know what to expect.[8]

For some, the caregiving responsibilities can become overwhelming, particularly when caregivers also have their own family and jobs, and the arrest of a brother or sister can become one crisis too many to manage.

Larry Stiller lived a simple life in a small assisted-living facility in Fort Lauderdale. It was one of a small number of group homes that were decent, clean, and well staffed. It was owned by a family who was well known in the community and cared deeply about their residents, who were vulnerable and in need of supportive services. Larry, in his mid-forties, had been diagnosed with both schizophrenia and intellectual disabilities. He loved his morning coffee and interacting with others around him. Larry had been arrested in front of a fast-food restaurant for allegedly "harassing customers for money."

"Judge Wren, I didn't mean to get arrested, I just needed some extra money to buy coffee," he said.

This was the topic of conversation each time Larry would get arrested. In fact, prior to these incidents Larry would go off his medication, but he never wanted to talk about that.

The first time Larry was referred to the mental health court, he sat in the jury box handcuffed to the high-back chair and nervously bounced up and down. With every anxious motion, he pleaded with me to call his brother.

"My brother, Mark, is at work. Can you call him . . . can you call him?" he asked repeatedly as tears ran down his face.

"Judge," Janis, the in-court clinician interrupted, "I think we need to send Larry to the hospital. He is not well."

I looked at Larry. He was tall and thin, with short reddish blond hair. He looked anxious. I thought that if I phoned his brother, it may help to calm him down and ease his anxiety.

"One minute, Janis, I know we're busy, but let me try to reach his brother," I said. "What's the number, Larry? Do you know it?"

I admit that after seeing the behavior Larry had exhibited in his previous court, I was surprised when Larry rattled off his brother's telephone number by heart and so quickly that I could not keep up. I asked him to please repeat the number for me, then placed the phone on the corner of my judge's bench on speaker mode. Larry started to perk up visibly. As the phone rang, Larry's enthusiasm began to boil over as he fidgeted in his chair and began to yell at the phone: "Pick up—come on—pick it up!"

It seemed as though the phone rang forever. Minutes passed, measured out by the steady, unanswered ring. Just as I was ready to give up, Larry's brother answered the phone. As soon as Larry heard his brother's voice, he squealed with delight. "Mark, its Larry! I'm in jail, again." And then, after a theatrical pause, "I'm sorry."

I took the phone off speaker and introduced myself to Larry's brother, Mark Stiller. I explained to him that Larry was in a specialized mental health court and was going to be transported to Broward Health (a system of hospitals and other healthcare facilities) for psychiatric evaluation and stabilization. I told Mark that the hospital case manager assigned to Larry would contact him when Larry was ready for discharge.

Mark was two years younger than Larry. When Larry was ready to be discharged from the hospital, the case managers arranged for Mark to come to the courtroom to pick him up and take him back to his living facility. As the two men stood before the bench, I saw little family resemblance between the two brothers. What was evident, however, was that Mark had gone through this process many times—perhaps too many times. His demeanor suggested that he was clearly miffed that he was in court again for what seemed like petty actions of his brother. Each time Larry was arrested, it was Mark who bailed him out.

"I love my brother—but *he won't stop* panhandling," Mark said, exasperated. "I have done everything that my parents asked me to do. I give him spending money, I buy him groceries, I take care of his out-of-pocket medical bills, I take him out when I can, I buy him clothes. It seems to me that when he gets bored or lonely, he walks to the shopping center near his facility and begs for money, even though he doesn't really need it." Mark paused, sighed, and shrugged as though he was working the words out of himself. He shook his head and met my gaze. "Judge, I'm trying to start my own business, and this is getting really stressful," he said.

"I understand," I replied.

I did understand. It sounded awful. Mark was in the prime of his life, trying to focus on his own responsibilities, and Larry was not exactly behaving like a team player. From his perspective, this was more than he bargained for or deserved. Janis and I offered several suggestions, such as a day treatment program or a consumer drop-in center not far from where Mark lived. At these drop-in centers, run by peers for peers, people with mental illness can visit and seek support, participate in social and recreational activities, and engage in self-advocacy and recovery-oriented activities. Larry responded to each of these suggestions by saying, simply, "I am fine where I am." It seemed that Larry had his routine and could not appreciate that his routine was landing him in jail and stressing out his brother.

Janis suggested that we follow Larry in the court and see how he does. Given the fact that he seemed otherwise happy where he lived, she did not want to "upset the apple cart."

I had a long talk with Larry in the courtroom that day about safe choices and good decisions. I am not sure whether he was capable of comprehending what I said, but I hope he heard some of it.

Larry was affable and fast talking, but I could tell he required a great deal of redirection and patience. He would drift off in the middle of important directions and seemed to disengage right when I, a clinician, or even his brother, Mark, tried to tell him something essential. I could understand and appreciate Mark's frustration.

Mark was married with two children, yet he dutifully embraced his role as custodian of Larry's affairs. Mark explained that their parents had passed away several years ago, and Larry became his responsibility. Even though it wasn't always easy, he said that he was fully open to continuing to care for his brother.

"Larry is fortunate to have a brother like you to support him," I said. I also emphasized that the court understood how challenging and at times overwhelming the caregiving role can be. Over the years we have met extraordinary brothers and sisters who have stepped up to take care of their siblings, with little fanfare and virtually no support or respite.

Thomas Capello had been arrested for resisting an officer without violence after he allegedly failed to produce his identification and show it to a police officer when the officer stopped him for drinking a beer on Fort Lauderdale beach and asked for his ID. Thomas had been diagnosed with bipolar disorder, and he was off his medications. The encounter became tense when he could not produce his identification. His brother, Jeffrey, appeared in court with him, and as they stood side by side, it was difficult to tell one from the other. They were identical twins.

Jeffrey explained that Thomas had been injured in a car accident when he was a teenager and had spent several months in solitude while he was treated at a local hospital. The traumatic brain injury had left him unable to live alone, as he had difficulty remembering things and needed help caring for himself. Fortunately, the injury was not worse, and there were many activities that he enjoyed doing.

"Sometimes Thomas forgets to take his medication," Jeffrey explained.

"Jeff and I are in business together," Thomas proclaimed in a proud voice. "We are cabinetmakers. Just like our father."

"That's true, Judge," Jeffrey added.

Jeffrey explained that his parents had been born in Italy, and their family had immigrated to New York when the twins were three years old. In the 1970s, the family relocated to Florida, where their father started a kitchen-remodeling business. I laughed to myself, thinking that is exactly what my family had done: my grandparents and other relatives decided to escape the harsh winters up north and build a new life in the Sunshine State.

Janis suggested that I order a psychological evaluation to determine Thomas's mental competency to stand trial. She speculated that the traumatic brain injury and resulting cognitive disabilities were significant and needed to be reviewed.

Over the course of several months, the Capello brothers came to court a number of times. Each time they were called to the bench, we marveled at the closeness of their bond and their deep sense of caring for each other. They were extremely fortunate that they had the family business together. They also gave special meaning to the phrase "my brother's keeper."

The concerns over what happens to an adult child with serious mental illness is often raised in mental health court. Many mental health court consumers are from single-child households or they are not close to their siblings. As the parents age, they can no longer provide the level of care that a mentally ill person requires, and often there is not a caregiving transition plan in place.

Not all siblings are willing to take on caregiving responsibilities. Some are weighed down by the burdens in their own lives and others are so estranged that they could not possibly act as feasible caregivers. Many may not have the financial resources or physical space to bring another family member into their home on a permanent basis. It is no small thing to care for the well-being of another person.

Within the next few weeks, I watched as the court deputies escorted in defendants for the mental health court docket. I heard Larry's voice even before he walked through the courtroom doors.

"Judge, I'm sorry, it's those police officers!" Larry yelled. "They have something against me—they hate me!"

"Larry is making choices, and they aren't good ones," Janis said, her voice heavy with concern.

"Well, we knew that Larry is extremely vulnerable in the community," I said. "What was I supposed to do, incarcerate him for hanging around a shopping center and asking for money? I knew that Larry would be at risk in the jail. That wasn't a solution."

"Larry, where is your brother, Mark?" I asked.

"I don't know, Judge. I haven't seen him in a while. I think he went to visit friends," Larry said.

Janis and I looked at each other, tacitly acknowledging that perhaps Mark was unable to continue supporting his brother. Perhaps he took a much-needed break or maybe he had moved out of the county. Janis offered to call him and at least try to confirm if he would pick his brother up. Clearly, some psychosocial strategies needed to be tried. Janis got on the phone and dialed his brother's number.

The line had been disconnected.

We did not have the heart to tell Larry.

"Let's talk about how we can help you, Larry," I said. "Let's talk."

CHAPTER 9

Changing Hearts and Minds

As we entered the ballroom of a major conference hotel in downtown Miami, I could feel the electricity in the air. In the five years since its founding, not only had the mental health court gained national prominence for justice innovation, but also its process was solidifying as we settled into our individual roles. It seemed to me, as presiding judge, as if there was a new wave of energy and understanding about the people whom the court was serving. We had not only begun to change the minds and attitudes about mental illness of the judges and lawyers in the community, but we also had grown through our own experiences, as witnesses to recovery and the boundlessness of human potential.

Based upon dialogues held in court, we learned that most people who have been referred to the court were high school graduates, had attended or graduated from college, and were working or had worked prior to their illness. It was fascinating to us how many people who had come through the court had attended some college or graduated with an associate's or bachelor's degree. Even when people self-reported that they were homeless or staying with friends, we asked about their former lives. No one, we found, is born without aspirations or dreams.

As our hopes and expectations grew, our sense of empowering court participants became stronger. We asked everyone, "What are your strengths? What is your vision for your life?" The deeper the questions, the higher the level of conversations and dialogues.

As presiding judge, I have seen that the depth of commitment to wellness and recovery has told the story of the court. Just as having the belief of another person can be the key to recovery, we found the court's belief in its clients facilitated the miraculous.

As the Broward County Mental Health Court celebrated its anniversary, the intensity of the public's response to the court and its work was overwhelming. Before long, new mental health courts were being established across the country. It seemed that in Broward County's quest to create its own court of refuge, our community had stumbled on a "tipping point of desperation," which, unexpectedly, exploded.

As news of America's first mental health court spread, the courtroom filled not only with mental health consumers, advocates, and their families but also with delegations from around the country and the world. Every day, mental health advocates from all disciplines scrambled to find space in the courtroom. When the seats ran out, news cameras and journalists lined the walls and recorded sessions, watching court proceedings unfold one after the other.

They all came with the same question: What was the court doing to promote mental health care over punishment and how was it doing it? The court answered this question case by case through its preservation of human dignity and its unconditional belief in recovery.

The court's growing reputation coincided with a growing sense of urgency for mental health reform, as Congressman Ted Strickland of Ohio sponsored legislation to establish pilot mental health courts. America's Law Enforcement and Mental Health Project Act passed the 106th Congress unanimously (the Senate in September 2000 and the House one month later) and was signed into law on November 13, 2000, by President Clinton. In 2002, I was appointed by President George W. Bush to the new Freedom Commission on Mental Health. A single community's call for compassion had led many—even policymakers—to question the conventional approaches of national and international law to mental health.

This fundamental change in criminal justice and mental health, spurred by Broward County's Mental Health Court, is greater than what can be measured in statistics such as the number of courts or mental health consumers served. Instead, the court sparked—and ignited—the idea that institutional change is possible if there is a will to fund adequate resources and commit to transform mental-health and behavioral-health care. This spark drove the proliferation of mental health courts across our country and others.

According to the Council of State Governments, today there are an estimated four hundred mental health courts, behavioral health courts, and other hybrid models across the United States and in several other countries. These courts function differently in different states. In Florida and other states, where healthcare budgets and spending on mental health are constantly being reduced, mental health courts connect consumers to limited community resources. In rural states such as South Dakota and Arkansas, where there are large pockets of poverty, mental health courts provide much-needed access to mental health care and treatment facilities through the referral process. In every region, however, mental health courts are a way to promote access to care, reduce incarceration, and promote accountability. Moreover, mental health courts have answered the need for a response to the national opioid crisis and its collateral impact on the criminal justice system.

In addition to these gains brought by the new mental health courts, one of the most tangible of our successes is the way the new court touched Broward County: in the twenty-first century, for the first time our county became a harmonious, tight-knit community. The mental health court itself was a rising star with its own homeless shelter, the Cottages in the Pines. The creative solutions created by the court were unparalleled.

On the heels of the court's successes, in 2001 I made a presentation about the Broward County Mental Health Court at a national mental health conference, to be held that year in Miami. I brought with me a woman named Rosemarie Stratton so she could share with conference attendees her experience with the court. My intention was to use this opportunity to humanize the court for the audience and showcase the experience of a mental health court consumer.

Rosemarie, thirty-four, had been diagnosed with schizophrenia and a co-occurring intellectual disability. Despite her challenges she was making great strides in her recovery and had established new goals of returning to school and work. Rosemarie had attended school up to the tenth grade, when she was diagnosed with a serious mental illness. Since then she had been evaluated under the Baker Act many times and had never truly engaged in mental health care for any sustained period. Rosemarie had been arrested for shoplifting at a local retail store and had been referred to the mental health court by her assigned division judge. After my portion of the presentation, I provided the audience with a summary of how Rosemarie was referred to the court and noted that she currently resided at the Cottages in the Pines, where several court participants had formed a supportive, rehabilitative community.

Rosemarie greeted the audience and took questions. She appeared confident on stage and spoke excitedly about her plans to return to school and to pursue a professional career in accounting. I was incredibly proud of her.

"This was one of the most exciting things I have ever done in my life," she told me after she left the stage.

When news of Rosemarie's appearance at a national mental health conference made its way to the executive team at the Henderson Behavioral Health Center, I could tell it represented a new milestone and ignited a new sense of pride and vision for the future. This was a milestone for the mental health provider stakeholders, particularly Henderson, which had lent the court a staff person to commence operation because the court had no funding to hire specialized personnel. It was a milestone for the members of the criminal justice and mental health task force that had met for several years without reaching consensus on what could be done to respond to streamline the criminal justice process for people being arrested with mental illness. And it was a milestone for the individuals and families in Broward County, that a modest local effort to try something to create a safety net to prevent or mitigate the criminalization of people with mental illness was having a positive impact on a local and national level.

Broward County needed to raise the bar in terms of recovery, and many mental health consumer activists in the community with ties to the Florida Department of Children and Families began to work toward formalizing a Peer Specialist Recovery Certification Program.

The foundation for US peer leadership and workforce development has its historical roots in the experiences and work of pathbreakers in the past. According to the consumer advocate Gayle Bluebird, the history of the consumer-survivor movement goes back to early pioneers such as Clifford Beers, a Yale graduate whose suicide attempt in 1901 led to his confinement in a psychiatric hospital. His autobiography, *A Mind That Found Itself*, published in 1908, ultimately led to the establishment of Mental Health America, now formally known as the Mental Health Association.[1]

The early certified peer recovery/peer specialist movement was led by Howard Geld beginning in the mid-1980s. According to his obituary in the *New York Times*, Geld, who died in 1995, got his nickname, Howie the Harp, from playing "his harmonica on the streets of Greenwich Village to earn money for food and a place to sleep."[2] He had written "proposals that led to $150,000 in financing from the state and other organizations for the Peer Specialists Training Center to train former patients to help others like them."

This served as an early model for the Mental Health Association's peer specialist certification and has led to an emerging US workforce where people with mental health problems, substance abuse issues, and physical challenges can legitimately work as a service provider in an integrated healthcare setting such as a mental health center, rehabilitation program, or supportive housing program. Not only does the ability to leverage one's lived experience in recovery offer the benefits of learning how to manage one's health from a "hands-on" perspective, but peer recovery support systems also promote social inclusion and break cycles of poverty for persons with disabilities by providing a ladder to financial independence and economic mobility.[3]

In Florida, peer recovery leaders such as Bill Schneider, Sally Clay, Patrick Hendry, Jeffrey Ryan, Tim Lane, and the members of the Florida Peer Network worked tirelessly to develop a forty-hour peer recovery specialist curriculum and certification process in the state of Florida.[4] In a program funded by the Florida Department of Children and Families, the Florida Certification Board administers the process whereby an individual can become a certified recovery peer specialist. There are three certifications: adult peer, family peer, and veteran peer. The Peer Support Coalition of Florida defines a certified recovery peer specialist as "an individual who self-identifies as a person who has direct personal experience living in recovery from mental health or substance use conditions, has a desire to use their experiences to help others with their recovery, is willing to publicly identify as a person living in recovery for [the] purpose of educating, role modeling, and providing hope to others about the realities of recovery, and had the proper training and experience to work in a provider role."[5]

In addition to a minimum of a specified number of years of "lived experience" for each category, individuals applying for certification must meet minimum educational requirements and complete a forty-hour training curriculum, which includes advocacy, mentoring, recovery support, professional responsibility, and electives.[6] Applicants must also provide documentation to support five hundred hours of related work or training, pass an exam, and comply with all other ethics and certification renewal requirements.[7] According to the Florida Certification Board, there are more than fifteen thousand certified peer recovery specialists in Florida. Their leadership has laid the foundation for an emerging consumer-centered mental health system in Florida, even as community systems of care in Florida, and around the country, continue to face budget shortfalls and reductions in services.[8]

The moment Sharon Nardelli was referred to the mental health court, in 2003, we began to alter our expectations of the population we anticipated to see. Sharon was a college graduate who, in her early forties, decided to take her shot at success in the entertainment field. Her dream was to become a recording star. Sharon had been arrested for disorderly conduct at a local nightclub. She had been diagnosed with bipolar disorder but was too busy to spend much time thinking about her health. Sharon was determined to break into the music field and spent a great deal of time trying to find work as a backup singer.

As Sharon herself remarked, she wasn't getting too far in South Florida, and her money was running out. Before too long Sharon found herself evicted from her apartment, and her mental illness was out of control and quickly turning her life upside down. Sharon's bipolar disorder had become unmanageable; she was swinging between extreme swings of "up" and "down." When she was manic, she described going on "adventures" that could last for days. When the depression hit, she barely could lift her head off the pillow of a couch that she slept on in a friend's apartment. By the time she was arrested, Sharon was emotionally and physically exhausted.

"I need help," she said in a strained voice that reflected her general fatigue.

There was a female bed available at the Cottages, and Sharon accepted it without hesitation.

Not long afterward, Sharon was joined by Margaret Smith. At forty-four years old, Margaret suffered from both post-traumatic stress disorder, stemming from childhood physical abuse by her mother, and an eating disorder. Margaret and Sharon were the same age and seemed to meet at an opportune time in life. Both women were single, at risk of homelessness, and extremely bright and vivacious. Margaret had been arrested for allegedly defrauding an innkeeper.

"I accepted a dinner invitation from a man I had met at a singles event," she said. The man said he was a financial consultant. He invited her out to dinner at an expensive restaurant on Las Olas Boulevard in Fort Lauderdale. Their first date seemed to be going well, but at the end of dinner, her date excused himself from the table.

"He never came back," she said. "It was one of the most embarrassing moments of my life."

When the waiter delivered the check, Margaret did not have enough cash or a credit card to pay the $196 bill. Margaret was aghast when the restaurant manager called the police. She was arrested on what became known as "the worst first date" anyone could have experienced. Later, that would become no surprise to me when I learned that Margaret had been a competitive tennis player when she was younger and relished a win any way she could get it. She told the story with so much conviction that we were transfixed. All the female lawyers in the courtroom began to shake their heads in disbelief as a sign of sisterhood and solidarity with Margaret's obvious humiliation.

At the Cottages, Sharon and Margaret established a community newsletter, the *Consumer News*, which included contributions from all Cottage residents. Poetry, favorite foods, essays, and a Community Events column was published every month. Howard Finkelstein's "Club Med for the Head" was thriving, and before too long the community was having an impact of its own.

So when word came from Henderson Behavioral Health Center staff that Margaret had had a psychiatric setback and her psychiatric status was not improving, the court personnel and members of the Cottages community were shocked and saddened. No one could have anticipated Margaret's health decline. I was not informed of the details, only that her psychiatric condition had severely deteriorated and that she needed to be hospitalized. She had been doing so well and was due to leave the Cottages and resume her life in the larger community. Some speculated that she may have been concerned about transitioning to more independent living in the community. Perhaps the thought of leaving the safety and security of the Cottages was too much for her consider. Whatever the cause of Margaret's psychiatric episode, she had immediately been admitted to the hospital and was under a doctor's care.

As I checked on her health status soon after her admission, I learned that she was not improving. I asked for the name of her treating psychiatrist and placed a call to him. Because of privacy rules I understood that the doctor could not provide any patient information to me, but I could provide him with information about Margaret that might help him to understand the direness of the situation.

I explained to him that Margaret is well known to the court and had been living at the Cottages for close to a year. I summarized Margaret's capabilities, talents, and love of tennis. But I could tell that her doctor was getting frustrated.

"Judge, the woman is *ill*," the doctor said. "She is diagnosed with schizophrenia, which means she is *ill*. What do you want?"

His voice carried such a clear tone of disrespect that I became incensed. I took a deep breath, forcing myself to pause. Perhaps the doctor was busy, but he did not seem to be listening to what I was trying to communicate, namely, that I cared deeply about this woman, and she was obviously not getting better.

"What do I want, Doctor?" I asked. "I'll tell you what I want—I want you to treat this woman properly and understand that she has been living an active and quality life! I want you to *treat* this woman so she isn't *ill* anymore."

I thought about Margaret's first court appearance and her story about being abandoned by her date at an expensive restaurant on Las Olas Boulevard in Fort Lauderdale. She had made such a lasting impression on the court. This was the first time I could recall hearing a diagnosis of schizophrenia.

I immediately called Pam Galan, a registered nurse and the chief operating officer of the Henderson Behavioral Health Center.

"I need your help on behalf of one of Henderson's mental health consumers," I said as soon as she answered the phone. I discussed my concerns with Pam, sounding more like a member of Margaret's family than a judge who had presided over her case. I suggested that a second opinion on Margaret's diagnosis was needed. This was a request that, as a judge, I have had to make when I feel additional advocacy is required. Providing such advocacy for those in need is a stated mission of the court.

"Let me review the situation and I will get back to you," Pam said.

I thanked her, but intuitively I had a negative feeling. I was not sure what had happened to Margaret, but whatever it was it seemed serious.

After a couple of hours, Pam called me back.

"Judge, I spoke with the charge nurse and reviewed Margaret's chart and the psychiatrist's orders," she said. "I believe that Margaret is being treated properly." Pam explained that Margaret was very ill when she was admitted to the hospital, and they were having difficulty stabilizing her.

My voice was breaking as I tried to argue with her. "Pam, please . . . is there any way to get a second opinion?" I struggled to hold back the tears.

"Judge, let me see what I can do," Pam replied.

Within a matter of days, Pam called me back. She wanted to let me know that she did arrange for a second opinion and that the reviewing psychiatrist believed Margaret's diagnosis and resulting treatment plan was appropriate.

That Friday, as soon as court was over, I got into the car and drove over to the Cottages. I did not announce my visit. I pulled into the long U-shaped driveway in front of the pale-green cottage that housed the administrative office. I just wanted to spend some time with the residents. I was sure they would be as concerned as I was about Margaret's status. The Cottages had grown into such an intimate, supportive community that it was almost like a family. And, like family, it was important to support one another.

When I entered the administration office, I learned that some of the residents were at group, and a few were working, but I took a seat in the living room and chatted with one of the staff members.

Within a few minutes, Sharon walked in. The look on her face told me that she was surprised to see me.

"Judge! What are you doing here?" she asked. "It is so great to see you."

"Did you hear about Margaret?" I asked. We sat together on the almond-colored couch and I updated her on my concerns and the information that I had received from Pam. Clearly, everyone was worried.

"I should show you what the residents have done for Margaret," Sharon said after I had finished speaking. Sharon led me outside and we walked down the pine-tree-lined block to the pink house on the cul-de-sac. There were four people to each cottage, and every home had its own identity, which reflected the collective personality of its residents.

When we approached Margaret's house, I could see the other residents had made a welcome-home sign out of colored soap across the front bay windows. When we walked in, there were personalized welcome-home notes and drawings hung on the walls around the living room area. A vase of homemade multicolor tissue paper flowers in a plastic vase sat in the center of the kitchen table.

I was overwhelmed but not surprised about the outpouring of love of the residents for Margaret. She had touched the lives of Cottage residents the same way that she had touched the lives of everyone in the mental health court—and the way she had touched my own.

Over the next few weeks I waited for news about Margaret's condition. I hoped to hear that her condition had improved and she was ready to return to the Cottages and resume her recovery activities and newsletter publications.

Within the next week, I received a call from Pam. She wanted to let me know that Margaret was not able to return to the Cottages. The doctors felt that she needed longer-term care, and her family had been located. They requested a transfer to a hospital on Florida's west coast. Pam told me that the residents of the Cottages have been informed, and they were planning a visit to see her to say goodbye. They collected all the cards, poetry, and drawings and were going to present them to her, wrapped in colored tissue paper. Sharon made a CD for Margaret of her recordings.

I never saw Margaret again. Her generosity of spirit and abiding belief in recovery lifted up so many people, and it underscored what the court had taught me about the resiliency of the human spirit. A little bit of Margaret echoes in a line that I often say to and about the court: "The rejection of stigma in favor of dignity is the essence of social justice."

CHAPTER 10

A Rush to Privatization

"Everyone knew this day was coming. But not this soon. And not this poorly thought out." This was how Michael Mayo, a writer for the *Sun-Sentinel*, began his August 8, 2011, column about the decision by the Florida Department of Children and Families to speed up the privatization of Broward County's mental health and substance abuse services by two years.[1] It was a decision made by the DCF Secretary, David Wilkins, without prior notice or consultation. Imagine: A major change is made in government policy about how you access your healthcare, and no one bothers to tell you or ask your opinion. No letter or public service announcement or news report was ever released. There were no community forums or town hall meetings to brief the public and seek input. As to criminal justice stakeholders, including mental health court judges, drug court judges, the sheriff's office, public defenders, state attorneys— absolutely no one had been consulted.

According to *Florida Health News*, hundreds of DCF layoffs together with severe budget shortfalls had accelerated the need for the state to relinquish its administrative and management functions to local entities.[2] As stated by Bob Sharpe, the former CEO of the Florida Council for Community Mental Health, "They can't monitor the existing contracts anymore and need these managing entities as fast as they can get them."[3] If there was any consensus, it was that "a rush to privatization could affect services in each area and how those who need them, would get access."[4] Given the dire state of mental health in Florida, it seemed logical that DCF, which had privatized Florida's Child Welfare System in 2006, would look to continue that trend.[5]

The DCF had begun to explore a new approach to the management of Florida's public mental health system as early as 2000. The reform would entail shifting DCF's administrative, management, and oversight functions to a nonprofit managing entity with which DCF would contract. *Florida Tax Watch* describes a behavioral health managing entity (BHME) "as a non-profit organization that manages a network of behavioral health providers in a specific region on behalf of the state."[6] In 2008, the legislature passed an amendment to Florida Statute 394.9082 that authorized the creation of behavioral health managing entities as a collaborative effort of DCF, the Florida Council for Community Mental Health, and the Florida Alcohol and Drug Abuse Association. The rationale for these entities is explained in the statute: "The Legislature finds that untreated behavioral health disorders constitute a major health problem for residents of this state, and substantially increase demands on the state's juvenile and adult criminal justice systems, the child-welfare system, and healthcare systems. The Legislature further finds that behavioral health disorders respond to appropriate treatment, rehabilitation and supportive intervention."[7] The thinking was that the behavioral health managing entity, as a local entity, would have greater understanding of the values, culture, and needs of the community. In this regard, a report on public management of mental health care sponsored by the Milbank Fund and the Bazelon Center for Mental Health Law notes that proper preparation and consultation with community stakeholders is essential for the effective management of a public mental health system reform, which includes experimentation with privatization.[8]

The 2008 financial crash ravaged state mental health budgets. In its 2011 report, *State Mental Health Cuts: A National Crisis*, the National Alliance on Mental Illness (NAMI) detailed massive cuts to non-Medicaid state mental health funding, which totaled nearly $1.6 billion, with deeper cuts to come. According to NAMI, state budget cuts impacted thousands of youths and adults living with serious mental illness. As a result of the cuts, several services were eliminated: critical community- and hospital-based mental health care, in addition to housing and access to medications. NAMI also projected that the loss of temporary Medicaid funding through President Barack Obama's stimulus package would end in June 2011.[9] The report states, "Medicaid is the most important source of funding of public mental health services for youth and adults, leaving people with mental illness facing the real threat of being cut off from life-saving services."[10] The report emphasizes that even under the best of economic times, funding for mental health is inadequate. The impact of an individual's inability to access care can be tragic, as we saw in the case of Aaron Wynn; the high-profile shooting of Congresswoman Gabrielle Giffords and murder of six people in Tucson, Arizona; and the Virginia Tech shooting in 2007. Clearly, there was an urgent need to find out what the plan was for Broward County.

As rumors swirled, I called Pat Kramer, Broward County's DCF director for adult mental health and substance abuse and asked her whether the rumors about privatization were true. "They are," she said. "I would be delighted to come and bring the judges and members of the criminal justice community up to speed on what is happening."

A meeting with Kramer was scheduled for August 5, in my courtroom, to officially air the current state of privatization in Broward County. I am not sure what the twenty-five-plus criminal justice stakeholders who attended were expecting to hear. But I am convinced that no one was prepared for what Kramer was about to reveal. Once everyone had taken their seats, Kramer thanked those assembled for taking the time to be at this meeting and addressed the audience.

She opened her remarks with four words: "The deal is done."

The deal is done? What deal?

I sat next to Michael Mayo, who as a journalist, one would think, would have had a heads-up if anyone had. But not even Michael had heard anything about the state's plan.

"Allow me to explain," Kramer continued, adding that although Broward County was slated to be one of the last counties in the state to be privatized, the secretary of the DCF had determined that due to unanticipated departmental budget cuts it was necessary to accelerate the plan. Further, it had been decided that it would be more expedient to merge Broward County with Miami-Dade County than to go through the time and expense of Broward's establishing its own separate managing entity through a competitive bidding process.

As Kramer concluded her summary, a voice came from the audience: "It's never going to happen." Surprisingly, the spontaneous utterance was mine. To this day, I do not recall having that thought. Perhaps it was my way of restoring dignity and respect to a community whose dedication to social justice and people with mental illness in the criminal justice system was—and is—linked to our identity and culture as a court system and county. Broward County, whose mental health system has been underfunded since the 1960s, to its credit has never given up. From the federal class-action suit regarding South Florida State Hospital to the high-profile case of Aaron Wynn, which ignited a grand jury investigation, to Broward County's Mental Health Court, it seems fair to say that Broward County's relationship to its mental health and substance abuse service systems runs deep. In fairness to Kramer, she was only the messenger. She spoke professionally and did the best she could.

As tensions grew, the group of criminal justice stakeholders tried to process what they had heard. Several people asked questions—but there were no answers. If a merger was to occur, no details were known. Kramer was not able to answer questions. She tried to convey a positive tone but had scant information. She clearly believed what she had said—that the deal was done and was in the process of being implemented.

In hindsight, perhaps my comment about the plan could have been more artful. I should have said that the process by which the citizens of Broward County have been treated, as evidenced by DCF's plan, was procedurally unsound. Further, it was unrealistic for the stakeholders in the room to accept this plan based upon the lack of the department's transparency and the lack of any meaningful opportunity for them to provide input. Had there been more consideration for Broward County from a procedural justice perspective, perhaps conflict surrounding the state's plan could have been avoided had the state been transparent and included Broward's stakeholders in its privatization planning process. Why is this important?

Procedural justice is the driving force in how people determine the legitimacy of authority. According to legal theorist Lawrence B. Solum, there are four elements of procedural justice, which I will illustrate by applying to the mental health court process.[11] The first and second elements of the process are related and are intended to introduce participants to the court. (1) To convey the substance of the process by underscoring the voluntary nature of the court with a humanistic tone. (2) To actualize the process by engaging and introducing the court's mission, goals, and values. This is the point where I express my support for the court participant and inform him or her about the court process and review due process rights and the voluntary nature of the court. (3) The integrity of process (an essential step) is to demonstrate that "fairness matters" because process is made up of rules and rules must be adhered to. (4) "The value of participation" is key to providing "voice and validation" so that a person perceives that he or she was "listened to" and the court's outcome is perceived as fair. This, in my view, is where dignity and empathic listening are keenly important.[12]

In mental health court, when a person voluntarily chooses to participate in the court, it is my hope that he or she does so because all people should believe they will be treated with dignity and respect and because they trust that the court's human rights mission of decriminalization and the promotion of mental health is legitimate.

Clearly, the lack of procedural justice in DCF's rush to privatization was a problem.

Within a week, Michael Mayo's column "Rushed Privatization Plan Will Harm Broward's Mentally Ill" was published.[13] Michael quoted Broward County's public defender, Howard Finkelstein, who commented, "It's going to make a bad system worse," and would result in a loss of scarce mental health dollars, which would be diverted to the managing entity and hurt community providers.[14] The controversial plan then caught the attention of Florida state senator Christopher L. Smith, who immediately convened a legislative hearing to find out why there had been no competitive bidding process for the managing entity. After several public forums, DCF secretary Wilkins reversed the plan and offered an "intent to negotiate" for Broward County to establish its own managing entity.

In October 2012, the Broward Behavioral Health Coalition was awarded the contract to manage the county's mental health substance abuse services. Its responsibilities would include a broad range of administrative and management functions such as contract management, system planning, oversight and allocating residential and treatment beds.

The lingering concern for me as presiding judge of a mental health court was, How would privatization impact the court process? In time I would find out.

When Joelle Dylan first appeared in court, it was a difficult and emotional hearing. Joelle was twenty-two years old and had been diagnosed with bipolar disorder. She had been cycling in and out of psychiatric emergency rooms for the past several years and self-medicating with drugs. She had never been connected to a mental health center. Joelle had been charged with criminal mischief for allegedly spray-painting her neighbor's mailbox. The arrest affidavit noted that Joelle told the police officer, "I thought the mailbox would look prettier if it matched the color of the house." She painted it bright yellow.

As Joelle was led into the courtroom in handcuffs and shackles, I noticed her mother sitting in the front row, on the side closest to the jury box. I asked the deputy to please seat Joelle in the chair closest to her mother. Joelle was petite and appeared much younger than her chronological age. She looked dazed and tired. In any other venue, Joelle could easily have been mistaken for a young teenager.

I asked her mother to approach the bench.

When she did so, I said, "Can you take her home, Mrs. Dylan?"

"I can't take her home, Judge," she said in a manner that reflected a deep level of frustration and angst. "Joelle will not take her medicine. And she is out at all hours of the night. I am worried sick—I just can't take it anymore!" After a brief pause, she added, "Joelle doesn't comply with her treatment, and I don't believe she ever will."

I thought carefully about how to address Joelle's mother. She appeared to be under extreme emotional distress.

"Mrs. Dylan," I said, "we can't give up on Joelle. I believe you are tired and afraid—which is more than understandable. Yet, if we don't have hope, we are hopeless. And there's no reason to give up on hope."

"What can I do?" Mrs. Dylan cried. "She refuses treatment."

"You know, Mrs. Dylan, there is a big difference between mental health treatment and engagement in treatment. In fact, Joelle has never been provided the services she needs to properly support her engagement in care. It's not her fault," I said.

Mrs. Dylan had been holding her arms tightly across her chest. Now she relaxed and unfolded her arms. She looked at her daughter, as she sat quietly in handcuffs several feet away from her. Mrs. Dylan's anguish appeared to lessen, as she realized that perhaps she had expected too much of her daughter. There was no way Joelle's mother could have known what Joelle's needs were. If only a treatment provider had taken the time necessary to talk with Joelle and her mother to determine what type of supports Joelle would need, they would have had a guide to show them how to navigate the system and how to secure those services.

"Please, try not to blame Joelle," I said. "She has not begun to engage in care, and we need to help her do that."

I glanced at Janis and knew she had already established a plan to get Joelle out of jail and into a residential bed.

"Judge, let me work on this. I have a few ideas," Janis said.

"What do you think, Joelle?" I asked. "Would you be willing to participate in a residential program to work on your health so you could feel better and enjoy your life?"

"Yes, I'm really tired of this, and I don't want to be in jail anymore," she said. "I want to participate in the court, and I will do whatever I need to do to be with my mother."

"Janis will come over and talk to you further and develop a plan."

As I prepared to call the next case, jail deputies led several male defendants into the courtroom. Each defendant wore a different colored jumpsuit: one gray, one blue, and one orange. The colors correlated to the jail site where each defendant was being housed. There was also one defendant in red. Red means that an inmate is under special precautions, a color commonly assigned to people with mental disabilities in the jail. Due to their preexisting disabilities, many individuals are unable to properly comply with instructions from a correction officer or are unable to manage their behaviors. According to the Broward County Sheriff's Office, approximately 40 percent of the detainees in the Broward County jail are diagnosed with at least one major mental illness and are prescribed psychotropic medications.

I looked at Allen, my court deputy, but he was already one step ahead of me. He called for an armed deputy to ensure the safety and security of persons in the courtroom. As the lawyers scoured the printed court dockets to see who had yet to be called, the defendant in the red jumpsuit was becoming agitated.

"Judge, why am I here? I'm not crazy!"

"Sir," I replied calmly, "I will be with you in one moment, please."

"OK," he said, as I located his paperwork.

His name was Raymond Collins. He had been arrested for allegedly causing a disturbance and for failing to leave the emergency room of a local hospital. I noticed that this was the fourth case referred to the court over the past several months that involved a hospital emergency room. It was a newly emerging pattern that I had begun to track informally since there seemed to be an uptick of incidents in emergency rooms leading to arrest.

"Mr. Collins, perhaps I am reading this arrest affidavit wrong, but were you arrested while trying to get medical attention at an emergency room?" I typically would not comment on the circumstances surrounding an arrest, but I felt it was important to understand why these arrests appear to be occurring with more frequency. The empathic tone of my voice seemed to take Raymond by surprise.

"Yes, Judge. I was trying to get a prescription for an inhaler because my property was stolen, and I need my medicine." Mr. Collins was fifty-nine years old and homeless. As I reviewed his criminal history, I noticed that he had numerous arrests for low-level and quality-of-life offenses such as trespassing, urinating in public, disorderly intoxication, and panhandling. I am not sure why he was wearing a red jumpsuit or what had occurred in the jail system.

"So, what is happening, Mr. Collins?" I asked. "How can I help you?"

Mr. Collins told me that he was from New Jersey. He was a veteran. "I was trying to see a doctor to get my inhaler replaced because I suffer from asthma," he said.

I explained to him why I thought his case had been referred to the mental health court: most likely the magistrate judge read the booking sheet and thought he needed assistance with services, particularly because the arrest involved a hospital.

Then, I counseled him about the use of the word "crazy." It was a minor thing, and perhaps I should have simply let his remark go and moved on. But I couldn't. It is my professional responsibility as a judge to create an atmosphere in my courtroom that is free of derogatory speech that is demeaning and in this situation could be viewed as stigmatizing. "Crazy" is such a word. The need to promote dignity necessitated me to say something about his use of the word "crazy."

"You know, Mr. Collins," I said, "I think you may understand that this division is a specialized mental health court and that there is a great deal of stigma and shame surrounding mental illness. And we do not want to use language that could cause people to feel badly about seeking mental health care.

"I'm sure you meant no harm, but for people affected by mental health conditions, that language could be hurtful," I said. "You know, a mental illness is no different than any physical illness, such as asthma."

"I'm sorry, Judge. I was upset," Mr. Collins replied. He cast his eyes to the floor and seemed genuinely remorseful.

By the conclusion of the hearing, Janis had coordinated a bed for him at Broward Outreach Center in Pompano Beach. This homeless center, run by the Miami Rescue Mission, has its own on-site medical clinic, where Mr. Collins would be able to get medical assistance for his asthma and access other services. I entered an order to have the Broward County Sheriff's Office transport Mr. Collins to the Broward Outreach Center.

Mr. Collins entered a plea of no contest to the charges against him, and I took judicial notice of his time in jail. As he walked out of the courtroom, he turned his head to look back at me and raised his shackled arms as high as he could in a gesture of appreciation.

Within a week, Joelle Dylan was back on the docket to discuss her residential program, answer any questions, and talk about her hopes for a successful and positive experience in what would mark the beginning of her journey to recovery and a new life.

"Judge," Janis said, "I need to talk to you to the side. We have a problem. Joelle was rejected from the program,"

"What do you mean?" I asked. "Everything was confirmed."

Janis informed me that she had just received an e-mail from the managing entity division, which oversees community bed allocation, stating that Joelle had been denied access to the community-based program she had been referred to.

"Why?" I asked. "For what reason would she be denied?"

Janis explained that DCF standardized procedures required that Joelle's assigned community case manager go to the jail personally and speak to Joelle face-to-face to obtain her verbal assent that she wanted to attend the program.

"But Joelle clearly stated in court that she wanted to go to a program. Isn't there anything you can do to get her into that program?" I asked.

"Joelle's bed was given to the next person on the waiting list." Janis sighed and paused before she said, "She lost it—the bed is gone."

Joelle's case had become a test of how the shift to privatization would impact the court's processes and how beds would be allocated to our consumers. As a result of privatization, residential treatment beds were controlled by the Broward Behavioral Health Coalition, and as a result, the court's diversionary process had been disrupted. A system called Level of Care Utilization System was creating new barriers in bed allocation that were preventing consumers like Joelle from getting the care they needed.

I took a brief recess and drafted an urgent e-mail to John Bryant, DCF assistant secretary for substance abuse and mental health. Bryant is a well-respected advocate for mental health and substance services and is supportive of the mental health court. I requested his immediate assistance to exclude the mental health court from this cumbersome and redundant process, which obviously was having an unintended negative impact on the court's diversionary process.

Within twenty-four hours, I received a response from Valerie Allen, the DCF mental health supervisor. Valerie and I go back more years than I care to remember, when we sparred during my time working for the Advocacy Center for Persons with Disabilities. Valerie called a meeting for within the week to discuss issues affecting the court and ways to streamline DCF procedures. These meetings are often intense for me, primarily because I am highly protective of the integrity of the court process. Sylvia Quintana, executive director of the Broward Behavioral Health Coalition, was present, along with several coalition staff members, who were young and eager to learn about the high-profile case of Aaron Wynn, Howard's letter to the grand jury, and how the court had been created.

At the meeting, after much banter, Valerie—who is always a strong mediator—offered suggestions that would provide the flexibility and autonomy the court needed to meet its diversionary goals. Janis would be given community case manager status, so that she could more easily make community placement referrals. This suggestion streamlined the process in terms of diversion from jail. No longer would it be necessary for community case managers to meet with individuals to verify what had already been determined through the court process. This simple change eliminated a critical barrier to jail diversion—and for this I was genuinely grateful. In the end, the ability to problem-solve is always about relationship and having the will to be flexible in the promotion of human rights, disability rights, and social integration.

Within weeks, Joelle returned to court with her case manager, Cynthia. Cynthia was extremely positive and had identified several of Joelle's strengths, such as her politeness, her altruism (she enjoys helping the other residents), and her love of music. Joelle is making steady progress and is slowly adjusting to the therapy groups and being around other consumers. Apparently, Joelle had been isolated at home and was becoming more detached from her family and friends.

It was an excellent report. I particularly appreciated that the program was flexible and that it allowed Joelle to be social when she felt the need to be around other people. The fact that she was adjusting to her medication and participating in activities was great progress. All of the staff were very proud of her.

"Joelle," I said, "I am so proud of you. In fact, we are all proud of you."

Janis said to me, "I know we experienced a few hiccups getting Joelle into the program. But I wanted to let you know that the managing entity worked very hard to contact treatment providers and identified a bed not only for Joelle but for the other individual who was more or less 'competing' for the same slot." Janis paused, before adding, "In this court we always talk about making lemonade from lemons. I believe this experience also helped me become more integrated within the DCF–managing entity sphere. Don't forget I was employed with DCF for more than twenty years. So, it is a win-win for all of us."

"I want to thank you," said Joelle. "And my mother asked me to tell you hello."

"Please tell your mother that I send my best," I said. Then, remembering the frustration and the hopelessness written on the face of a parent who believed her child would never get any better, I knew I needed to say one more thing. Despite the lack of services, Joelle's mother had held on to the hope the court had told her to have. And now, Joelle was getting better. I smiled and looked at Joelle, who stood before the bench with a positive future in front of her. "And please tell her that I am proud of her."

CHAPTER 11

In Honor of Our Elders

One morning, Andrew Lanius, the prosecutor for the city of Hollywood, Florida, came into the courtroom to share an unusual case with me. "I have a case in another division that might be more suitable for your court," he said. The case involved an elderly woman named Mary McCullough, who was living in an RV with no running water or electricity. She was charged with two separate misdemeanor counts of cruelty to animals for dogs, her pets, which were suffering from dehydration and malnourishment due, in part, to Mary's living conditions. As I read through the details of the case, I wondered if I could also supply a referral to Broward County Elderly Services to assess the habitability and risk of harm for Mary. After all, the court has a long-standing relationship with Elderly Services, whose case managers do incredible work on behalf of vulnerable older adults.

"I was wondering if I could bring Ms. McCullough over to the court now, since she is in the building and has no transportation?" he said.

Even though I questioned the appropriateness of the case to my court since there was apparently no mental health finding, there was no harm in hearing what the defendant, Mary, had to say.

At the very least, perhaps the court could refer her to a service that would prove useful. "Sure," I replied. "You can have her come over along with her attorney."

Within minutes, the city prosecutor, the special public defender, and the defendant arrived. The prosecutor handed me a four-page arrest affidavit, two competency evaluations, and an order from the judge, which found the defendant, Mary McCullough, mentally incompetent to proceed. Ms. McCullough had been charged with two separate misdemeanors counts of cruelty to animals.

The allegations were disturbing. Animal control investigators alleged that Ms. McCullough lived in an RV camper without electricity and running water. The dogs had been observed by animal control officers to be severely malnourished and dehydrated and living without proper ventilation. Since that time, the dogs had been removed from Ms. McCullough's residence and taken to emergency care.

"So, what is the problem?" I asked. "What is the city looking for this court to do? Shall I refer her to Broward County Elderly Services?"

"This case is a bit unusual," said Andrew. "Ms. McCullough lives in an RV in the parking lot of a retail drug store. She is seventy years old, and the city does not wish to arrest her. We just want to her to find a decent place to live. But she refuses to leave her camper, which we believe is unsafe. We were hoping you could order her into treatment or something to resolve this situation. Additionally, we are concerned that she will bring more dogs into the RV."

Since this wasn't an obvious issue of mental health, I was unsure as to how the court could intervene in this matter and asked Mary McCullough and her attorney to approach the bench.

As they took their place at the podium, I introduced myself and explained to them the nature of the court. I emphasized that this is a court of social service.

"Can you tell me a little about yourself?" I asked Ms. McCullough.

I noticed that she was well groomed and stylish. Her blond hair was coiled into a neat bun. She was wearing a geometrically patterned retro-style dress that looked like what someone would have worn in the 1960s. She appeared to be a bright and gregarious character. She explained that she had been one of the first airline stewardesses in the United States to fly transatlantic flights for Pan American. She told the court that her life "was in the air." She had never married and enjoyed living in her RV because, she said, she felt more secure in smaller spaces.

"What an exciting life you have led, Ms. McCullough! You are quite a pioneer for women in your field," I said.

I asked Janis if she would take Ms. McCullough and her attorney outside in the hallway to speak to her about her needs and find out how she was truly faring.

When they returned, the hearing resumed. Janis took the lead.

"I have spoken with Ms. McCullough, who does not believe she requires any mental health services or social services of any kind. She explained to me that she is very comfortable in her RV. There is a bed area for her to sleep, and she purchases food and water from the drug store and does not wish to move." Janis paused before adding, "Essentially, Your Honor, Ms. McCullough is an urban camper. If anything, her conduct may be viewed as eccentric. She has made a lifestyle choice—kind of like a hippie. She is a free spirit."

I turned to Andrew Lanius, who had listened to Janis's option. "Well, it appears that Mary is free-spirited," I said. "What would you like this court to do?"

"Why can't you order her to see a therapist or take medication?" he asked.

"That would not be legally appropriate. Even if there were a mental health condition, Ms. McCullough has the right to make her own healthcare decisions. Moreover, I do not believe you can medicalize every problem," I replied.

"The city attorney is very concerned that she will acquire more animals once this case is closed. She refuses to agree not to bring more animals into the RV—otherwise the city would dismiss the case."

Ms. McCullough's special public defender, who worked for the city, stood to address the court. "I believe this case must be dismissed, Your Honor. The city cannot prosecute this case, and my client is not a danger to herself or others and not subject to involuntary treatment under Florida law."

"Mr. Lanius," I said, "defense counsel is correct. What can this court do?"

"All we are asking is that you work with her to ensure that she understands that she is not permitted to house animals in the RV and to help the city negotiate a more suitable place to live."

This request seemed reasonable. I turned to the defendant, who still appeared as bright and gregarious as she had been when she first entered the court. "Ms. McCullough, are you listening to what the city prosecutor is saying?" I asked.

"Yes, Judge, but I love my dogs. I took good care of them, and I do not agree with the city."

I understood the city's concern. This situation was vexing and it was apparent that some sort of intervention was necessary. I just wasn't sure what that intervention would be. It was clear that, without Ms. McCullough's agreement to move out of her RV, the consequences of forced action by the city to evict her would leave Ms. McCullough homeless, and the experience would be extremely traumatic for her. Whatever was going to happen, it would be preferable to have Ms. McCullough join the decision-making process and take part in her own solution.

"Mr. Lanius," I said, "doesn't the city have housing resources and case managers you can contact to explore what supportive housing options may be available?"

"I'm not a social worker. I really don't know the answer to that."

"Counsel," I said, "we are all social workers. It is part of the job."

I agreed to keep the case and continue to work with Ms. Mc-Cullough to explore what housing options would be available. I asked Janis to check with Adult Protective Services to determine whether they had assessed this case and then set the next court hearing.

"Judge," Mr. Lanius said quickly, "I am sorry, but I have already placed several calls for housing resources. No one in the city was able to assist me."

The court was silent for a moment, and I considered the next course of action. I called a quick ten-minute recess to consider the available options.

When the court reconvened, Janis immediately said, "I was able to find out some information regarding Ms. McCullough." Janis had found out that Ms. McCullough had a closed case with both Adult Protective Services and Broward County Elderly Services. Apparently, when the APS investigator and Elderly Services case manager went to check up on Ms. McCullough in her RV, she refused to let them in. Slamming the thin little door with the tiny square window and miniature blinds, she said firmly that she did not want their help.

"You know, Judge," Janis added, "these agencies cannot provide services if someone refuses assistance."

I placed my head in my hands. I wanted Ms. McCullough to know that we needed her cooperation to help resolve this situation before it turned into a crisis. I did not want her to end up living on the streets, like many other elderly adults without resources.

According to the National Coalition for the Homeless, the number of elderly adults at risk of homelessness has increased throughout the country.[1] In 2016, the *New York Times* reported that according to the most recent data from the Department of Housing and Urban Development, homelessness among our nation's elderly has increased by 20 percent.[2] Per the report, from 2007 to 2014, there were 306,000 people over fifty living on the streets.[3] In South Florida, the combination of a lack of affordable housing and deterioration of health and finances has led to a critical housing shortage. The *Palm Beach Post* reported in June 2014, "There are nine seniors waiting for every occupied affordable housing unit."[4] In Broward County, the need for affordable housing is equally dire. As of February 2017, the Broward County Housing Authority stopped accepting applications for Section 8 housing, noting that three thousand names are already on the waiting list.[5]

I lifted my eyes to look at Mary McCullough and sighed.

"Ms. McCullough, I am sorry, but you can't stay in the RV," I said. I hoped the empathy I felt somehow flowed into my voice so that I could communicate how much I understood and how difficult this was for her. "I know you think it is safe, but it isn't." I watched her face for signs to show me whether she agreed with me or not. I saw nothing to guide me, so I continued. "As a former flight attendant, you know better than any of us in this courtroom that safety always comes first. I know, with all of us working together—along with the social workers at Broward County Elderly Services—we will find you a place to live that is not too large, with water and electricity so you can be comfortable and live with dignity."

I waited for a response—a protest, maybe. Or a nod. Anything. When none came, I continued, "You deserve that, Ms. McCullough. And I am sure the city will dismiss the charges if you would agree to move out of the RV, move to safer housing, and do not possess dogs."

Ms. McCullough took in a sharp breath and stood still for several seconds. I watched her facial expressions as emotions and thoughts flickered across her face. Concern, fear, hope: They resided in her eyes and on her cheeks for seconds before they flashed away with another thought or feeling. As I watched, the emotions settled, and she seemed to settle along with them. She might well have realized: *This problem is not going away. And things can get considerably worse if the city intervenes and I do not agree to accept services.* The life that she wanted would surely be taken away.

"Well, Judge," she finally said, "I will try to cooperate. And if the social workers can find me someplace small and tidy"—she nodded her head, perhaps searching for an image of a home to replace the one she had called her own for decades—"I will agree."

The court turned silent. The sound of shuffling paper, of muted conversations, of footsteps in the hallway seemed to stop for the woman who was asked to give up the only home she knew and who—in the interest of health, safety, and humanity—had done so.

After a human eternity, she added, "You know, Judge Wren, throughout my entire career, I always took great care of my passengers. Some became good friends. I really loved them."

A life lived in the air might have held mystery and magic—but it was a lonely life, I realized, as I watched Mary McCullough walk away from the bench.

————————

"Judge," the public defender interrupted, "I would like to call a case; my client is getting antsy."

An elderly couple, Mr. and Mrs. Tramm, approached the bench. Mrs. Tramm was seventy-six years old, extremely petite, and spoke very little English. Although her husband could speak English, it appeared as though Mrs. Tramm preferred to address others—in this case, the court—in her native Mandarin. Mitchka Bavandi, an assistant public defender, had ordered the services of a Mandarin court interpreter, who appeared at the bench with them.

Cultural sensitivity is essential in a highly diverse community such as Broward County, where in 2010 the non-Hispanic white population shrank to less than 42 percent of the total population.[6] Those concerned with the promotion of mental health must deal with the fact that different cultural beliefs about mental illness influence how individuals and their families perceive mental health treatment and whether they will seek care. For those who do want care, overcoming existing barriers and disparities in services available to different socioeconomic and cultural populations are additional considerations one must keep in mind.[7] Some resources may be, simply, out of reach as a result of economic or cultural factors.

For older court participants, the importance of all dimensions of culture—language, sexual orientation, gender, education, religious or spiritual orientation, class, race, and ethnicity, the personality traits it takes a lifetime to hone—are magnified. Those are the distilled elements that for elder court participants can either enhance or derail a mental health plan.[8] The elderly hold lifetimes of accumulated experiences and wisdom; these invisible traits represent the imprint of a person. They can also contain the details that can derail an ill-conceived treatment plan.

Several decades earlier, Mrs. Tramm had been diagnosed with schizophrenia. Because of their culture and beliefs, the Tramms did not want her to take medication. Instead, the public defender explained, Mrs. Tramm had been treated with Chinese herbal remedies.

I reviewed her case file. She had been charged with petit theft: pocketing paper napkins and a pack of chewing gum from a corner market.

I introduced myself to Mr. and Mrs. Tramm and informed them about the mission of the mental health court. Mr. Tramm explained to me that he was the owner of three Chinese restaurants in Broward County, and that his wife had worked with him in the restaurants for nearly all their married life. "She is doing fine," he said.

Mrs. Tramm appeared highly agitated. She stood next to her husband clutching a stack of what appeared to be random papers, each one covered with Chinese characters printed in red ink and also bearing some food stains. She blurted out something along the lines of "being a Supreme Court Justice."

"Judge, if I may," Janis said, stepping forward. "I spoke to Mr. Tramm prior to court this morning."

Janis explained that the Tramm family was very supportive and protective of Mrs. Tramm. She had never been left by herself for any length of time. The Tramms' large extended family worked in their restaurants and also had shared the responsibility of caring for Mrs. Tramm.

Len, the prosecutor, weighed in. "Judge, that may be true, but I would like you to see the defendant's criminal history. This is certainly not her first criminal offense."

Len handed me Mrs. Tramm's criminal history. I was surprised to see that she did in fact have several prior offenses for petit thefts. Granted, most of the charges had been dismissed. But the list wasn't short, and it spanned several years.

Mrs. Tramm heard the prosecutor's comments translated by the interpreter in Mandarin and became increasingly excitable. She began to respond in a manner that even the interpreter could not decipher. Her arms flapped rapidly, moving the scraps of paper in her hands like little white wings. Words intermingled with moans and sighs.

"I suggest, Your Honor, that we follow Mrs. Tramm in the court for a time," Janis said. "We can see if the court's engagement interrupts her justice involvement. I will work with Mr. Tramm to strengthen the supervision that the family provides for her."

Janis led Mr. and Mrs. Tramm to a seat in the second row, where they could observe the court process as Mrs. Tramm became calmer.

This would become her favorite pastime. For months, there Mrs. Tramm would sit, transfixed by the lives moving in and around the courtroom. It seemed to soothe her somehow.

As presiding judge, I never imposed any conditions to her release other than her family's promise that she would commit no new offenses—which, incredibly, she didn't. For six months she attended mental health court hearings, observing them from her spot in the second row, with her husband by her side.

One day not long after the Tramms started observing my courtroom, the double doors to the courtroom burst open and two police officers walked in holding the arms of a frail, elderly woman who had been arrested in her bed. The woman was in her eighties, and her eyes were wide open and filled with fear. I immediately stopped the hearing and halted the officers who had brought her into the courtroom before they could sit down.

"What have you done?" I asked.

"Judge," one of the police officers replied, "this woman is under arrest for battery, and due to her advanced age, my supervisor suggested that we bring her to your court."

I asked them to be more specific. "What do you mean 'arrested for battery'?"

"Well, Mrs. Wilson is a resident at Paradise Gardens Nursing Home," said one of the police officers. "And according to the nursing staff, she allegedly bit the cheek of the nurse who was attempting to feed her."

"What?" I asked in disbelief.

I immediately dialed the telephone number of the nursing home and asked to speak with the administrator from the bench. When I confirmed that I had the administrator on the phone, I told him that I had Mrs. Wilson in my courtroom and that I was sending her back to the nursing home "forthwith!"

The administrator, who obviously detected the outrage in my voice, conceded to my demand. He agreed that Mrs. Wilson should be returned to the facility.

"Officers, you heard me: please transport Mrs. Wilson back to her nursing home," I said. "I expect that this case will not be prosecuted, and my clinician will be following up with the nursing home to review this matter."

Mrs. Tramm, in the second row, listened intently.

One dimension that is rarely mentioned in discussions of our courts relates to vulnerabilities of our elder court participants to elder abuse: physical or emotional abuse, neglect, and financial exploitation. According to the Centers for Disease Control, elder abuse is a serious problem and often difficult to detect. Many individuals who may have been subject to abuse do not report the abuse out of either fear of reprisal or shame or because of a disability, so they cannot.[9] In fact, in 2008, one in ten elders over the age of sixty reported emotional, physical, or sexual abuse or neglect within the previous year.[10]

Within days, Janis informed me that she had reviewed the issue with staff in accordance with my court order, and she would conduct an inquiry into this matter. According to Janis's findings, Mrs. Wilson had been diagnosed with dementia. She also had other serious medical problems that required skilled care. To make the situation more egregious, at the time she was arrested, she had a feeding tube inserted in her stomach, which meant she was not capable of feeding herself. I thanked Janis for the updated information. She replied that the matter has been turned over to the Agency for Health Care Administration for review.

For the next few moments, the courtroom remained silent, as if in disgrace—or perhaps it was in gratitude that even if the police did not use their discretion properly, Mrs. Wilson did not end up in jail. Instead, the case came to this court first, where it was halted, just as it should have been. With that acknowledgment, I called the next case.

Richard Martinez, sixty-seven years old, had been arrested for stealing food from a grocery store. The arrest paperwork alleged that Mr. Martinez had been seen by the store's loss-prevention staff eating various food items in the store while pretending to shop. His "shopping snacks" included a container of clam chowder that he had taken from the self-serve soup counter in the deli section, a package of freshly made sushi, and a fountain soda. When the deputies wheeled him into the courtroom, it was evident that his needs were far greater than hunger.

"Mr. Martinez, sir," I said, "how are you doing?"

"I'm sorry for eating what wasn't mine," Mr. Martinez responded. "I was hungry, and I could use some help."

"What's going on in your life that led you to take food from a grocery store that you couldn't pay for?" I asked.

Mr. Martinez explained that he had worked in construction most of his life. In 1997, he fell off the roof of an office building he had been working on. The fall resulted in a coma that lasted for several months. "You could look it up, Judge," Mr. Martinez said. "It's true, and it was in the news."

I asked my judicial assistant, JoAnne, to see if she could find the news report. As JoAnne went to her laptop to do an online search, Mr. Martinez continued his story: "The doctors put a metal plate in my head and after I'd been released from the rehabilitation center. But I still wasn't able to work due to the severity of my injuries and brain trauma." He explained that the pain had been so intense that he turned to alcohol and drugs to manage his pain. Then, as often happens in a medical crisis, Mr. Martinez's wife left him. He lost everything as a result of his disabilities and his growing addiction to drugs and alcohol.

"Judge, I found the article," JoAnne called from her impromptu work station in the court room. "It was published in the *Miami Herald*." She handed me a copy of the article, which confirmed that Mr. Martinez had survived a horrendous accident. It was a miracle that he had survived a fall from the roof of a four-story office building that had been under construction in Fort Lauderdale.

"You certainly are a lucky man," I said to Mr. Martinez as he sat handcuffed in his wheelchair, next to the jury box in the courtroom. "I mean, to have survived such a serious accident."

Mr. Martinez hung his head in a way that suggested he did not share my view of his good fortune to be alive. "I have nothing to live for," he said. "I have nothing: no home, no family, no health insurance, and now the doctor tells me that I could lose my left foot because of the lack of circulation in my leg." He pulled up the left pant leg of his jail jumpsuit and showed me his leg. It was abnormally swollen and colored black, as though ink had been injected into his leg. The sight was disturbing, and I had to look away.

"Judge, if I may," Janis said as she approached the bench. "Mr. Martinez appears severely depressed, and I suggest you order him to Broward Health based on his medical history. It is clear that he is at risk of harm on the streets, and his medical needs are complex."

I nodded assent. "Mr. Martinez," I said, "I am going to get you out of jail and we are going to try to find you a place to live."

"Bless you, Judge," he said.

I had a long history of advocacy on behalf of clients who resided in South Florida assisted-living facilities (ALFs), nursing homes, and other institutional settings. As a former public guardian and attorney for the Advocacy Center for Persons with Disabilities, I had personally observed and reported countless horrendous incidents of elder abuse, exploitation, and neglect of Florida's most vulnerable citizens. For people with psychiatric and physical disabilities who need supportive housing and services—because they are not able to live independently and properly care for themselves or live with family—housing options are significantly limited.

For those who are without financial resources, ALFs are often the only alternative to homelessness. Because of the poor housing conditions, many people are reluctant to live in an ALF and would rather endure the harsh conditions of the streets to those associated with group living, where abuse and inhumane living conditions are the rule rather than the exception. In mental health court, referrals are rarely made to ALFs, and if such a referral is unavoidable, consumers are referred to only a small handful of known providers.

When Mr. Martinez had been discharged he appeared more optimistic and reported that he was feeling better. The hospital social work department had negotiated a bed for him at a local ALF of which the court was not aware.

There were other reasons why it was hard to find a home for Mr. Martinez. I immediately called the hospital's social worker and learned that Mr. Martinez received only a monthly $700 Social Security disability payment. He had no other income. The hospital caseworker stated that "it is almost impossible to secure housing placement for a person who receive[s] that minimal amount, and that many facilities will not accept people who rely on wheelchairs."

I conferred with Janis. Her opinion was that unless Mr. Martinez qualified for a skilled-care nursing facility or an Adult Disability Medical Home, the hospital social worker was correct.

I entered an order for Broward Sheriff's Office to transport Mr. Martinez to the ALF that had been arranged for him. I decided to monitor the case, not because I was concerned about re-offense but because I did not have confidence in the discharge plan and wanted to follow Mr. Martinez into the community and monitor the appropriateness of his placement and make sure that he had a safe place to live.

Within weeks, Mr. Martinez was back in jail. He had been arrested for trespassing. Allegedly, he had been sleeping on the lawn in front of a bank. When the deputies wheeled him into the courtroom, we were eager to find out what happened. So far, reports had been a blend of mystery and rumor.

"I got to the facility," Mr. Martinez said, "and the next day I was taken by staff to the Social Security office. They dropped me off and left me there. I had nowhere to go."

I was incensed. Who drops off and leaves a disabled person who had endured severe physical, mental, and emotional trauma? I had my concerns about this ALF, and I suppose things could have been worse. At least he had not been harmed.

I redirected my frustration to action. "Janis," I said, calling my court clinician to my bench, "from my experience it is impossible for people who receive less than one thousand dollars a month in Social Security to secure a placement in a decent assisted-living facility. Is that so?"

Janis reminded me of the elderly woman who was diagnosed with schizophrenia and living in an ALF when there was a fire. Fortunately, she had been hospitalized at the time of the fire and was not in the building. "You and I went to see that facility," she reminded me. "We immediately contacted the mental health center that was responsible for her case management to investigate further."

That story triggered horrible memories of my experiences at several ALFs and group homes during my tenure with the Advocacy Center for Persons with Disabilities. In 1994, when I was the plaintiff's monitor of the federal class-action suit *Sanbourne v. Chiles*, a significant portion of my time was spent following class members into the community to evaluate the appropriateness of their community placement in accordance with their discharge plan from South Florida Hospital.[11] The Florida legislature had been threatening to close the state hospital. My monitoring duties covered six counties. Although it was not feasible to follow every class member, I did review the living conditions of many of our clients. For those without families, the living conditions were often substandard and, depending on the facilities' deficits, required a range of legal responses.

In 2011, Carol Marbin Miller and the *Miami Herald* investigative team published a three-part series called "Neglected to Death," which revealed the egregious and inhumane treatment of adults with disabilities residing in ALFs throughout Florida.[12] The series also documented the impact of failures to hold these facilities accountable through mandatory inspection schemes and effective enforcement of state laws designed to protect the health, safety, and welfare of vulnerable Floridians. The *Herald* series had great impact and resulted in the closure of dangerous homes, the punishment of repeat violators, and the passage of tougher laws.[13]

Yet for Richard Martinez and other older Floridians in need, it was not enough. Resources to enhance existing assisted-living programs and establish new models of care still have not been embraced by state policymakers.

Eventually, Janis successfully negotiated a bed for Richard Martinez in an ALF where the care was of good quality and she had confidence in the owners.

"Every now and again I get lucky," she said, referring to the fact that Mr. Martinez had survived such a tragic accident and then had survived an episode of poor care that had impacted both his body and his mind.

We called the next case—Mrs. Tramm. It had been six months since her case had first come to the attention of the mental health court. I asked the prosecutor if he was satisfied that the family had stepped up its supervision of Mrs. Tramm. New protective rules had been implemented among the family members so that Mrs. Tramm was carefully supervised while shopping and was not permitted to shop by herself.

"Are you ready to dismiss the charge against Mrs. Tramm?" I asked the prosecutor.

"Yes, Judge. I think the Tramm family has done a good job in helping prevent any further problems or arrests," he said thoughtfully. "I will dismiss the charge."

It proved to be a bittersweet goodbye. Everyone in the mental health court enjoyed Mr. and Mrs. Tramm's presence in the second row, listening and watching. We were uplifted by their devotion to each other and the quality of life that they were living in their golden years.

"Please visit our restaurants. We would be happy to have you," Mr. Tramm said.

As they walked away from me toward the courtroom door, Mr. Tramm wrapped his arm around his wife. It was a gesture of grace and kindness acquired over a lifetime. Perhaps that is the true wisdom that comes with age and experience, and that is the wisdom that we, as a community, must learn to protect and honor.

CHAPTER 12

The Power of Human Connection

In a court where the people who come before it are often living on the edge, our approach is to problem-solve one step at a time. After all, the last thing a healing court wants to do is add to the stress load of people who are already overwhelmed by life itself.

Pam Hendricks, the behavioral health coordinator for Broward Health, referred Kenneth Marks to the Broward County Mental Health Court. A former baseball player in the major leagues, Ken, twenty-three, had been arrested for disorderly conduct and trespassing for allegedly failing to obey a police officer's order to leave a nightclub a week before. He had subsequently been diagnosed with schizophrenia by a psychiatrist at Broward Health. He was scheduled to appear in court this morning, along with his parents. I had no idea what to expect.

As I walked into the courtroom, I was relieved to learn that only a handful of cases were on the docket. I thought, the fewer people the better, since I did not want the courtroom to appear too intense or chaotic. I scanned the courtroom for Ken. He was not difficult to spot: young, athletic, and tanned from his hours of play and practice in the field, he sat alongside an older couple—his parents. Ms. Hendricks's initial report indicated that the family was having a very difficult time handling the news of their son's arrest and subsequent schizophrenia diagnosis. From the expressions on their faces to the way each seemed to cling tightly to the other, it was abundantly clear to me that the parents were in shock and in deep emotional pain.

As I took the bench, I intentionally walked slowly and remained silent. The court staff followed my lead and waited for me to open the proceedings. I asked Janis to please introduce herself to the family and take the time necessary to explain the court process to Ken and his family and to let them know that their son had been referred to the court by the behavioral health staff at Broward Health.

After his arrest, Ken had been able to call his parents from the jail, and they had paid the required bond for his release. From there, they had driven him directly to the emergency room at Broward Health for an evaluation. After a week of observation, Mrs. Marks told Janis, "The team physician informed us that Ken had not been himself." The team sent Ken home and notified his parents that he had to be psychiatrically evaluated. His parents blamed themselves for his arrest because, as it turned out, they had already scheduled an appointment with the family doctor. Unfortunately, the arrest occurred before the appointment with the physician.

They tortured themselves wondering whether the arrest could have been avoided if only they had scheduled an appointment earlier or had taken their son to an emergency room immediately upon his return home from training. Maybe the arrest would never have happened. They had so many questions: Why did this have to happen to their son? Would he ever be able to resume his baseball career? "He worked all of his life to get to play in the big leagues. It was his dream. And now it's gone," his father said in a broken voice.

As Kenneth Marks approached the bench, I was surprised that he had achieved so much at such a young age. He appeared dazed, and I speculated that was most likely from the medication and all that he'd experienced over the past week.

"Ken," I said in a mild tone, "welcome. I understand that you have been through a great deal, and I am not going to prolong the hearing this morning."

"I am OK, Judge," he said. "I am up to it."

We spoke about the court, and I listened to his parents explain that Ken had been recruited from college and had just signed with his team. Ken's father gasped for breath as he noted that Ken had not been playing too long before his mental health began to deteriorate.

We talked for a few more minutes about where Ken would receive care. His mother had contacted a private psychiatrist who had been recommended to the family. A follow-up appointment had already been scheduled by the case manager at Broward Health.

"I think that is enough for today," Janis said. "Let's allow Ken to get some rest. He will come back next month, and we'll evaluate his progress."

I thought that was a reasonable suggestion under the circumstances. As the deputy clerk prepared the court notice for the next hearing, Ken's mother asked if she could speak to me for a moment. She stepped toward the front of the bench and said, "Judge, we are worried that now that Ken is away from his team, he will become more depressed and lonely."

I reassured her that Ken was going to recover and live a fully active and engaging life, but he needed a chance to get used to his treatment. I promised her that we were going connect him with additional services and peers so he would not feel alone, if he was interested. Granted, I wasn't yet exactly sure what those supports would look like, but I bet that physical fitness, healthcare, and baseball were on the list.

At the next scheduled hearing, once again Ken appeared in court with his parents. They indicated that things were going all right at home, but that it was "going to be a long road back to health." I could tell the family was still in shock and were trying their best to be strong for each other.

As the hearing continued, Ken said that he had played baseball in college in South Florida before he transferred to another university in Texas. He talked highly of the coaches who had mentored him and hoped to get back to the game that helped him to feel truly alive, he said. As he spoke, I reflected on the many mental health consumers I knew who had been diagnosed with a serious mental illness and gone on to reclaim their lives and accomplish tremendous goals.

During the time that Kenneth Marks was a court participant, I was honored by an appointment by President George W. Bush to serve on the New Freedom Commission on Mental Health, established in 2002.[1] The commission was a part of the president's New Freedom Initiative, which was intended to advance the progress of the landmark legislation of the Americans with Disabilities Act, legislation that President George H. W. Bush had signed into law in 1990. The New Freedom Commission on Mental Health would convene every month to take testimony from the public and from experts and to engage in a comprehensive study and review to evaluate how best to improve mental health in America. The commission was charged with the responsibility of submitting both an interim and final report to the president.

As I boarded the plane from Fort Lauderdale to Washington, DC, to attend one of the monthly meetings, I was seated next to a tall man. Eventually, we struck up a conversation. He shared with me that he was a college baseball coach. Ken's last court hearing was on my mind, and my curiosity was piqued. The chance coincidence that I would find myself sitting next to a college baseball coach when Ken had just described his happiness at playing college ball—and the strong relationships he had formed with former coaches—stirred something in me. I decided to continue the conversation.

Not wanting to ask him his name, I introduced myself. Then, he told me the name of the college where he coached, and I knew that this was no ordinary meeting. This might offer me a chance to get some help for Ken.

We spoke for a while, and I told him what I did for a living and about the mental health court. I wondered how I could ask for his assistance without revealing Ken's identity. As the pilot announced that we had begun our descent for landing at Ronald Reagan Washington National Airport, I realized that this was not a coincidence, and I needed to say something before it was too late.

"Sir," I said, turning to the coach beside me, "I was wondering if perhaps you could assist me."

He nodded and said, "Sure."

"There is a wonderful young man in my court who played baseball in college. He is having some challenges, and I know that if he had the chance to speak to you . . . that perhaps you could offer some words of encouragement to him and, who knows, offer him some advice and guidance about how to hold on to his love of the game and remain engaged in baseball."

"I would be delighted," the coach replied. "I once had a baseball coach who promised every player that, no matter what happened in life, he would always be there to support and encourage them. He inspired me to do the same."

I watched as the coach dug into his brown leather carry-on bag and handed me his business card. As I examined it, I thanked him. I could not believe my luck. *Yes, it is him, Ken's former coach!* I did not say anything about this to the coach, though, due to confidentiality required by the court.

After the weekend, I was eager to return to work and share the story of this chance meeting with the court staff. I did not know for certain whether Ken would feel comfortable reaching out to his former coach, but that would be his choice.

Soon after I returned to Fort Lauderdale, I was advised that Ken had had a mild setback and had been readmitted to the hospital. I realized that my surprising news would have to wait. The court dockets seemed to be growing longer with each session. Perhaps it was because judges and lawyers were becoming more aware of people with mental health issues in their own court divisions and wanted to give their clients the opportunity to participate in my court.

One day a special guest attended the court: Jamie Fellner, senior counsel for the United States Program of Human Rights Watch.

She was visiting the court as part of a national survey and investigation into the criminalization of people with mental illness in the US. It was a great honor to have Human Rights Watch, one of the world's most prestigious and effective global human rights and social justice organizations, in the Broward County Mental Health Court.[2] The fact that Fellner was focusing on the criminalization of mental illness in the US certainly suggested that the organization had identified the criminalization trend in America as a human rights issue that was in dire need of attention and action.

It was an intense and high-energy docket, as Fellner sat near me, in the witness box, to observe the court process. Since the court was a teaching model, I explained the principles of therapeutic jurisprudence as I went and emphasized the human rights elements that were embedded in the court process. This included the fact that the court was voluntary, highly individualized, and operated on a pretrial basis. The court did not require a plea of no contest in exchange for participation, which meant that the individuals retained their constitutional right to trial, should they choose to opt out of the court and return to the criminal division, to which they had originally been assigned.

I emphasized to Fellner that I rarely applied sanctions in the court and only in those circumstances where noncompliance posed a public safety risk or if there was a re-offense that required remanding a participant to the jail. Typically, in the event of noncompliance, further action would be determined on a case-by-case basis. After a reasonable effort to promote engagement, an individual's case would either be transferred back to the original court division for case administration or would be taken care of by a plea bargain in the mental health court. The importance of procedural justice and the minimization of the coercion was a hallmark of the mental health court. Early evaluations on the court were led by Dr. John Petrila of the University of South Florida and Louis de la Parte of the Florida Mental Health Institute, in partnership with the MacArthur Foundation, and yielded the outcomes that Howard Finkelstein and Broward County's criminal justice and mental health partners had worked so hard for: "Researchers noted, 'The

Broward court was designed to be informal, often involving inter-action and dialogue between the participant about problems and treatment options. . . . The patience and tolerance . . . create an impression that speedy disposition of a large number of cases is not a priority."[3] In the early years of the court, Professor John Monahan, when he presented the findings of the preliminary observations of the court across the country, even went so far as to say that participation in the court was almost as pleasant as "going out for an ice cream sundae."[4] In other words, court participation was not only voluntary but also, and primarily, therapeutic.

Within a matter of weeks, Ken returned for a status hearing in mental health court. Once again, he appeared with his parents. This time he shared the good news was that he was feeling better. His doctor had made an adjustment to his medication that significantly improved how he was feeling.

Janis reviewed his progress and was pleased. As the hearing continued, I reached down into my purse and pulled out the business card that I had received from his college baseball coach. I thought about how I was going to explain this serendipitous experience. After considering several possibilities, I decided that the best way to raise it was simply to reveal the facts and circumstances as they occurred.

I appreciated the change of roles: Now, I was the storyteller.

I started off by explaining that the most amazing thing happened when I flew to a meeting in Washington, DC, about a month before. "I sat next to a very nice man who was tall and had a mustache and we engaged in conversation. As we shared our line of work, he told me that he was a college baseball coach."

I handed the business card to my deputy and asked him to give it to Ken.

As Ken examined the card, his face registered surprise. "What is this?" He stared at the card in disbelief, blinking fast and hard. When he looked up, his eyes glistened under the courtroom lights. "Did you really meet my coach?"

"I did," I replied. "I want you to know that I never mentioned your name to him or revealed anything about the fact that you were a participant in the mental health court. What I did tell him was that there was a wonderful young man in my court who had played baseball in college, and he may appreciate getting a bit of encouragement and having someone to talk baseball with."

Ken was overwhelmed with joy. "You mean I could call him and just say hello and catch up?"

"Absolutely," I said. "He said that he would be delighted to speak to this young man. Think how surprised he will be when he finds out it's you."

Ken's mother and father were overwhelmed. I explained to them that I did nothing more than take my seat in the plane. It was really a matter of fate. As soon as I uttered those words, I thought about Aaron Wynn and how, at the court's celebratory launch, Howard Finkelstein had referred to the creation of the court as a leap of faith.

"You know," I said, "I bet if you were interested, you could ask your coach about how to go about volunteering as a baseball coach at one of the colleges here in South Florida." I watched Ken's expression, which lingered on the edge of disbelief and overwhelming joy. "Only when you're ready," I added.

In the months that Ken and his family came to mental health court for their hearings, I found myself thinking about baseball and how it so elegantly articulated the importance of human connection and support. Beyond the mundane details—a game played in nine innings with nine players on each team; beyond the sport's alliance with American culture as a "perpetual drumbeat keeping time through American history"—something about the interaction of the players themselves underscored what I witnessed in the mental health court each day.[5] Perhaps it was the centrality of home plate— an apt metaphor for the importance of home and family—and the way "success" is often reliant upon the people one is surrounded with, paired with stable and safe living conditions. The hearth, the home fire, and family gatherings at holidays, happy memories of home, often form the inner layer of fortitude that mental health activists refer to as "resiliency." Home: the place of origin and the place we perpetually return to, like the runners scattered across first, second, and third bases who all hope to cross home plate.

But it wasn't just the home-plate metaphor. Listening to professional games on the radio on my drives to and from the courthouse, I realized that baseball was a game that consists of a series of second and even third chances. It takes three strikes for a player to be called "out," and there are three "safe" bases a player can take refuge on to avoid being "tagged out." It takes three "outs" to turn a team from defense to offense. And in any professional game, there are at least nine innings. It is a choreography of opportunities regained.

Baseball, in other words, isn't a game that demands a single act of perfection. Instead, it is a game that acknowledges the human condition as one riddled with chance and failure.

Ken's face lit up as he read the name on the card again and again. Just like the game he loved, life had offered him up second and third chances.

Violet Harrison had been arrested for disorderly intoxication at a popular bar on Fort Lauderdale Beach. At thirty-two, Violet didn't quite look like the kind of person who would be arraigned for the reason she had been. She was diminutive—or, perhaps, diminished. Drawn into herself, her posture seemed to collapse as Allen, the court deputy, escorted her into the jury box.

"Vi, we're here for you! We love you!" Violet's mother called from the first row of spectator seats where she and her other daughter sat. Allen made a beeline for Violet's mother to admonish her to maintain decorum in the court.

"Mrs. Harrison, please do not yell in the courtroom," I said firmly. "That is not appropriate."

The noise in the courtroom dropped to a murmur, then silence. Both Violet and her mother wore wounded expressions on their faces as though I'd taken something away from them. It was an expression I've seen in the court before—the expression of people who believe they have lost everything.

I wondered what this family had been through.

I called Violet's case immediately so her mother wouldn't have to wait and become more anxious. I introduced myself to everyone, appointed the public defender for Violet, and began to gather some basic information to find out why she had been referred to the court.

"Hello, Violet," I said. "Before we begin our conversation, is it all right if I ask your mother a few questions?" This was a part of the court's process—allowing defendants like Violet to maintain their constitutional rights. Anything a defendant says could be used against them in prosecution. If Violet's case were to be transferred to a court in the criminal division, her legal rights must be protected. That is also why everyone who participates in the mental health court is appointed an attorney.

Violet nodded in response and said quietly: "Yes, you can talk to my mom."

I turned my attention to Violet's mother, who approached the bench. "Can you tell me anything about your daughter?" I asked.

"Judge," Mrs. Harrison said, "my daughter is full of life and very talented. She used to dance and loves to cook. She has a heart of gold." She took her other daughter's hand, to compose herself.

"It's just . . . that," she said in a low whisper, "a very bad thing happened to Violet when she was in college." Her words broke apart as she began to sob. She tried to control herself by taking deep breaths, but her body shook as tears rolled down her face. While I waited for Mrs. Harrison to regain her capacity to speak, I learned from Violet's case file that Violet had been diagnosed with post-traumatic stress disorder and bulimia. After a few moments, Mrs. Harrison regained her composure and went on. "Violet rarely leaves the house anymore. She has a few girlfriends that she still sees, but they have been a bad influence on her."

"Mom, that is not true!" Violet said forcefully, standing up.

"All right," I said. "We all need to take it down a bit." I turned my attention to the in-court clinician. "Janis," I said, "I am interested in your thoughts."

"I would rather not get into Violet's trauma history other than to say that she is connected to a private therapist in the community who she likes very much. I am not sure what to suggest, given her insurance coverage and the fact that she has positive family support."

"Violet," I asked, "what are your goals? I understand you were in college. What degree were you pursuing? What was your vision?"

In a clear voice, Violet told the court that she had been studying to be an art therapist. "Once, I had a passion for art and children." Her voice drifted as if she was talking about a different life. She had been enrolled in the school of education at a local community college but had dropped out after the traumatic event—Violet had been the victim of date rape. Since then, Violet had languished and was unable to engage in her life in any real way. She lacked the energy and the desire to return to school. For Violet, life had become a struggle to cope with mental health issues that were well beyond her capacity to understand, let alone control.

But after this pause, Violet pulled herself together and started speaking again. "It makes me feel bad to always have to rely on my mom for everything. I mean, I should be able to get out of bed in the morning without crying. I should be able to go to class without becoming so scared of what might happen to me there. I should be able to know when and how much to eat. But I can't. . . . I just can't do any of that."

Violet's mention of how disappointed she was that she had not overcome the problems in her life while she spoke about managing her mental health challenges inspired me. She acknowledged that she needed to learn how to manage her own care better and not rely on her mother to do so. In fact, this idea is very close to what social workers and therapists call health activation, which is an important idea buttressing what we attempt to do in the mental health court. I learned about health activation while attending the American Case Management Association's Behavioral Health Leadership Conference in 2015.[6]

Health activation is a widely recognized concept of engagement for patients with chronic medical conditions such as diabetes, mental illness, obesity, and cardiac disease.[7] Its goal is to teach self-care skill building that leads to lifelong engagement in personal wellness. The research indicates that the more a patient is engaged in his or her health, the better the health outcomes, and that to activate one's health, one needs to shift one's focus to positive lifestyle choices and healthy living. This can include any number of things, such as improving one's physical fitness, following a healthy diet, getting adequate sleep, engaging in meaningful social activities, and spiritual pursuits. The higher the level of health activation, the more effective one's healthcare management.[8]

What if I made health activation a priority in the Broward County Mental Health Court? I thought for a moment about the possibility before I decided I was ready to roll out a new court initiative to counter critical loss of mental health programs. Mental health court participants would need to step up in terms of taking responsibility for their own healthcare management and learn how to be advocates for themselves.

I asked Janis to explain health activation to Violet and her family. On the basis of the literature, Janis had prepared an example of a self-care management plan. In addition to making her therapeutic appointments each day, Violet would create her own structured wellness plan. It would include activities such as healthy living practices that she enjoyed doing and that would help her manage her PTSD symptoms and her eating disorder.

In addition to getting sufficient sleep, the plan would focus on eating nutritiously and engaging in physical activities and other pastimes that Violet had once enjoyed doing and would make her feel better. She would not be allowed to consume alcohol. To deal with her eating disorder, Janis suggested that Violet try an Overeaters Anonymous support group or a twelve-step women's support group to help her manage the stress of facing the challenges of an eating disorder alone. Janis also suggested if Violet liked to paint, garden, or write, that time be set aside for such creative activities. Spiritual activities could also be part of Violet's program—for example, meditation, yoga, or other spiritual or faith-based activities that would foster feelings of gratitude and of being a part of something greater than herself.

As Violet listened to Janis's explanation, she seemed to become more alive, more vibrant. Color seemed to return to her skin, and she smiled when Janis finished her explanation. In fact, she was ecstatic.

"Judge," she said, obviously excited, "I used to love tap dancing when I was a kid. And I used to love to try new recipes. I guess all of that just sort of stopped." She paused as if collecting her thoughts. "Anyway, my mother has been suggesting that I eat more of a vegetarian diet. She has been reading about the benefits of diet and mental health. But I've always wanted to learn how to bake and decorate cakes. I think I might take a class on that."

After Violet's hearing, the court advocated for everyone to create their own wellness plan. Health activation became a core component of the court process. The celebration of health—of life—became, in some respects, the modality of the court. Perhaps it was no accident that I designated the mental health court a "Zero Suicide Initiative Court."[9] My decision came in part from reading about the recent surge in suicide rates across the country. To celebrate life was to keep it safe. And the court would do just that through its dedication to suicide prevention, which would now come under the court's broadened health activation banner. Safety planning information would be distributed from the bench at every hearing, including the numbers for local crisis hotlines and the National Suicide Prevention Lifeline.[10]

Each new court initiative built on the last. Life is sacred, and to guard it would require preventative and therapeutic measures to treat not only body but mind, heart, and soul.

Within a few weeks, Violet and her family returned to court for a follow-up hearing. They were pleased to be back in court, now that the family's circumstances had improved. Violet was dressed in a floral dress with purple, red, and orange flowers. She, like the flowers on her dress, seemed vibrant and alive.

"Judge, I brought something to show you," she said the moment she walked into the courtroom. It seemed that Violet had embraced health activation with both arms and soul. She had prepared an elaborate demonstration board that included a large multicolor diagram with illustrations linking her daily and weekly health activation activities to specific health goals. It was a work of art.

Illustrated with tasteful images clipped from magazines and books and loose sketches in watercolor that she herself had made, the plan specified her scheduled activities: dance, journaling, meditation, spiritual reading, and a power nap.

For her evening activities, she was going to prepare dinner with her mother, bake, practice yoga, and watch a few favorite shows with her family until bedtime, which was at 10 p.m. Her chart included a separate section for therapeutic appointments, highlighted by positive life affirmations and therapeutic goals. It was all written carefully in vibrant ink in a script that looped pleasantly around itself in beautiful spiral flourishes. Drawings of flowers and musical notes floated to form a loose, organic frame as if holding the plan together. It was as though Violet was signing the document with who she was and who she wanted to become.

When Violet concluded her description of her "health activation project," the entire courtroom applauded. I am not an expert in health activation, but by anyone's standards, Violet's efforts demonstrated something remarkable and beautiful.

Just when I thought Violet's presentation had concluded, she had one more surprise up her sleeve. She shared with me that she had signed up for the Whole Health Action Management (WHAM) Peer Specialist Training, offered by the National Council for Behavioral Health.[11] This program would allow Violet to take her lived experience in her own health management and integrate it into the WHAM program. It was a program developed by peers for peers.[12]

Health activation has been a positive addition to the court's recovery toolbox, but it did not address the community's lack of available residential treatment beds and housing options that were the result of a standardized level-of-care screening process and the bureaucratic allocation of available bed space. How do we provide for those who have no family or who do not have the support and backing of their family? How can the court find a way to help?

Just a few days before Violet's presentation, I received a call from Fran L. Tetunic, a professor of law and the director of the Dispute Resolution and Restorative Justice Law Clinic at Nova Southeastern University's Shepard Broad College of Law. She asked if we could meet to discuss how the clinic could serve the court. The clinic works across diverse areas of the law (juvenile justice, child welfare, family law, guardianship) to promote alternative dispute resolution and was interested in expansion of its scope. I scheduled a meeting immediately. My vision was to leverage the services of the clinic to expand the support network of the court and help people in mental health court find their way home.

CHAPTER 13

A Crying Shame

Derrick Brown and his father, Tyrone, stood before the bench at a status hearing to review Derrick's community placement. At twenty-two years old, Derrick was intellectually disabled and had been diagnosed with attention deficit hyperactivity disorder (ADHD). He'd just been released from the Miami-Dade County jail, where he had been held after a series of elopements—running away—from residential treatment centers to which he had been ordered. I didn't understand why the judge decided to release Derrick to his father's care. Tyrone Brown had just been released from prison after serving twelve years for robbery and hadn't seen his son for well over a decade. Perhaps the judge didn't realize that Derrick would need specialized care for his condition, or perhaps he didn't realize that Derrick's father would be incapable of providing that level of care, given his limited resources and experience as a parent.

The last time Tyrone Brown had seen his son, Derrick was a ten-year-old boy who loved to play basketball and video games and do all the other sorts of things one would expect a young boy to do. To Derrick, his father was a stranger, a reminder of lost childhood memories, of holidays and birthdays. Perhaps Tyrone appreciated this—or perhaps not. Derrick, however, stood close to his father as if he were a lifeboat and the court, an endless ocean. For Derrick, his father was one of two adults he trusted, a trust that had formed through the father-son bond, as tenuous as that was.

"It is nice to meet you, Mr. Brown," I said. "It was good of you to be here today."

Tyrone Brown lowered his head and stood remorsefully before the court. Although he was not the subject of the hearing, one would have thought, seeing his body language and other non-verbal communication, that he was the one facing a tribunal for punishment.

"Judge," Mr. Brown said, "I have failed my son, my family, and, most of all, myself. I have come to ask for the court's forgiveness and help. The last time I saw my son . . . he was very different. I have been away in prison for so long. I feel like I am living on another planet. I don't know how to operate a smartphone. I have no idea how to transact for basic services, and I do not have a steady job. How could I possibly take of my disabled son when I can barely take care of myself?"

"I understand, Mr. Brown," I said. "I do not believe that the judge who released Derrick to your care had been properly informed about Derrick's special needs."

Derrick had been referred to the mental health court three years before on a charge of trespassing and possession of cannabis. Since that time, the court had made numerous attempts to secure an appropriate community placement for Derrick. So far, every placement had failed, and Derrick had often run away.

For the past six months, Janis had been monitoring Derrick at a group home in Miami-Dade. We had been told that everything was going well when, in truth, Derrick had been cycling in and out of jail in various locations in Florida. It took a great deal of effort, but we had finally gotten Derrick back to Broward County.

At this point, the court was at a loss. Derrick's impulsive behaviors had proved too much for even the most experienced program administrators in Broward County, including Dr. Samuel Kelly of Dynamic Health Care. In the past, every time the court requested help to divert Derrick out of jail, Dr. Kelly had always stepped up to the plate. This time, however, he asked the court to allow him to step out. Ansom Phillips, the criminal justice liaison for Florida's Agency for Persons with Disabilities, was also present at the hearing.

Dr. Kelly opened by saying, "Judge, I asked for this hearing because I am greatly concerned about the health and welfare of Derrick who has been placed in one of our therapeutic group homes."

"Can you be more specific, Dr. Kelly?" I asked.

"Yes, Your Honor. We care about Derrick very much. At this point, I believe our program has exhausted every reasonable behavioral approach and strategy available to us. To sustain Derrick in our program, the state provided him a mental health technician to support him on a one-to-one basis. This means that this staff person's sole responsibility is to support and assist Derrick. Yet this strategy has not been effective. Derrick has walked away from the program each day. As you know, this is not a locked facility. Staff cannot legally force him to stay or restrain him. Our case management team believes that he is more interested in walking around the neighborhood in search of drugs than he is on working on his rehabilitative goals."

"Judge," Ansom Phillips interjected, "in anticipation of this hearing, I have contacted the director of the Agency for Persons with Disabilities for assistance in identifying a group home which is equipped to manage Derrick's intellectual and behavioral challenges anywhere in the state of Florida."

As Derrick listened to the discussion surrounding his fate, he became increasingly agitated.

"Miss Ginger, I want to stay with Dr. Kelly," he said. "I'll be good—please, Judge Ginger."

As Derrick's pleas become louder and more intense, I covered my face with my hands, as if that would shield me from the emotional intensity of the hearing. It was difficult to witness Derrick on the verge of tears, pleading for the only life he'd known. I wondered when—or if—a solution could be found. I told myself over again in a silent mantra, *Every problem—no matter how vexing—has a solution.*

I directed my attention to Mr. Phillips. "What do you propose?" I asked.

"In my view, the search for an appropriate residential placement for Derrick must be widened," he said. "In the meantime, Derrick is at risk. His elopements have led to at least half a dozen arrests in two different counties. I cannot ask Dr. Kelly to continue to try to maintain Derrick in his program. We must consider the other clients who reside there, who are vulnerable. I also believe, based on Derrick's behavioral pattern of elopement and substance use, that he is at significant risk of victimization by adults with criminogenic behavior. I believe he should be remanded to the jail for his safety and the agency should expand its search for community placement."

"I am very concerned about this proposal, Mr. Phillips," I replied. "This court is dedicated to decriminalization—putting Derrick in jail is not consistent with the values of the court. There *must* be some other alternative than jail."

"If I may," Janis said. "We need to be objective about how we respond to this dynamic. Derrick will not meet criteria for hospitalization. I know this is a terrible situation—but someone could get hurt or worse." Janis paused and crossed her arms over her chest before releasing a deep sigh. "I don't think I need to remind you about the recent shooting in North Miami, which involved a case manager of a young man with autism who walked away from his group home. When his case manager ran after him, the police received a call about a man with a gun. It was tragic! There was no gun—it was a toy truck. The case manager knew that his client loved trucks, and he carried one to help stop him from running. Somehow, the police mistook the toy truck for a gun and shot the case manager. Fortunately, he survived. But the young man with autism was traumatized and ended up institutionalized.[1] This incident was devastating for everyone. We don't want something like this to happen to Derrick or his caretakers."

"That's very true, Janis," I said quietly. "We do not want to invite tragedy."

As I contemplated the possible solutions I could offer Derrick, my mind wandered to the recent Miami-Dade County shooting of twenty-five-year-old Levar Hall. According to news media reports, Mr. Hall's mother had called the police because Levar (who had been previously diagnosed with schizophrenia) had been behaving erratically. She told the 911 dispatcher that her son had just been released from a psychiatric unit and was not stable. When the police arrived, they found Levar Hall armed with a broomstick. He was shot and killed when he failed to comply with police commands.[2] As difficult as it was, I knew I had no choice but to concede that tragedies surrounding police encounters can occur. Until an appropriate home for Derrick could be found, he would be safest in jail.

"Judge," Ansom Phillips said, "I will do everything I can to locate a more appropriate placement for Derrick as quickly as possible."

I glanced at my court deputy as he instructed Derrick to take a seat next to the jury box. Derrick understood what was happening to him and began to shout, "Judge, I'll be good—I'll listen!"

I did my best to reassure him that he would not be staying in jail for very long and that we were going to find him a place to live where he would be happy and safe.

"No, Judge, I want to live with my father!" Derrick cried. His voice, desperate, was weighted heavily with loss.

I scanned the courtroom for Tyrone Brown, but during the hearing Derrick's father must have quietly slipped out. He had not said goodbye to his son or tried to comfort him. Unable to emotionally absorb what had become of his son and not able to help, I suppose Tyrone Brown thought it best to leave.

I could not imagine what Derrick was thinking when he, too, noticed that his father had left him there in the courtroom to fend for himself against people he hardly knew—and against an uncertain future. Children of incarcerated parents have difficulty trusting others, including their parents, once they emerge from behind bars. For Derrick, it must have been heartbreaking to have invested trust in a father he'd hardly known and to have been rejected so cruelly, so suddenly, and so publicly. The courtroom's silence reflected my wordless shock back to me. The truth is that for Derrick and other young minority men referred to the court, the social determinants of where one was born and raised, what kind of adversities were experienced in childhood, including poverty and parental neglect—all of these intersect in the criminal justice system.

To date, statistics across the country reveal that the majority of incarcerated teenagers and adults are from minority populations in the lower income bracket. It's no surprise, therefore, that the complex relationship between racial and class bias and disparities in health, in a highly fragmented and underfunded mental health system of care, often frustrates the court's goals to extend services to those who need them most. Instead, system limitations coupled with negative cultural attitudes place obstacles in the way of breaking the cycle of arrest, leaving substandard housing, poor education, adverse childhood experiences, neglect, exposure to violence, and incarcerated parents to give rise to behavioral problems that a community-based approach could, in time, ameliorate.[3]

Currently, more than 2.3 million people are incarcerated in our nation's jails and prisons.[4] Approximately 50 percent of all inmates in US jails and prisons are black, although they make up less than 13 percent of the population.[5] More startlingly, one in six inmates has a diagnosable mental illness.[6] The development of an accessible and culturally competent system of mental-health-care delivery is essential. Research reveals, however, that the development of health policy is often the responsibility of those with little representation of the black population or health professionals who are knowledgeable of the culture of African American communities, committed to their well-being. [7]

In 2001, the US surgeon general, David Satcher, published *Mental Health: Culture, Race, and Ethnicity*, a supplemental report to the landmark 1999 report *Mental Health: A Report of the Surgeon General*. The supplemental report responded to the fact that although the United States is a diverse nation, rich in "incalculable energy and optimism," it is essential to emphasize the point "that all people do not share equally in the hope of recovery."[8] As the surgeon general stated in the 1999 report, "Even more than other areas of health and medicine, the mental health field is plagued by disparities in the availability of and access to its services. These disparities are viewed readily through the lenses of racial and cultural diversity, age, and gender."[9]

The supplemental report also documented the existence of disparities that impact the mental health care of racial and ethnic minorities compared to nonwhite populations. Findings include a lack of access to and availability of mental health care and services. Further, even if mental health care is secured, the care is often of poor quality. According to Satcher, minorities are overrepresented among the nation's most vulnerable populations, minorities have higher rates of mental health disorders, and the "burden for minorities is growing."[10]

What happens when rehabilitative programs, services, and supports are not available? For many people—depending on their level of care needs, culture, and other psychosocial factors—sometimes what is being offered in mental health courts holds little relevance for lives that have drifted off course. This, paired with family dysfunction or economic struggle, makes not only locating care but truly engaging in care extremely difficult. Ken Marks, the young baseball player, had the support of his parents to assist his journey toward recovery. Derrick—like many other young people without caregivers—was forced to face his journey alone, leading to a life trajectory filled with trauma and adversity.

Watching Derrick stand before the bench after his father had abandoned him illustrated what the research has clearly shown: without necessary family and community supports, recovery from mental health and behavioral health problems is a nearly impossible struggle.

Kelvin Wesley grew up in Fort Lauderdale. He had been a stellar athlete, excelling especially in the 400- and 800-meter races in track and field. He had been arrested for the offense of criminal mischief. According to his arrest affidavit, Kelvin allegedly threw a rock through a store window. Kelvin had been referred to mental health court by his public defender.

Kelvin appeared in court accompanied by his mother. Janis spoke to his mother prior to the hearing. Mrs. Wesley explained that Kelvin came from a large family that was deeply involved in their church. His mother had raised three other children and worked two jobs. "I do the best I can," she said in her meeting with Janis. She worked as a home health aide for two separate organizations, which meant she often had to work nights.

"Kelvin was always a sweet boy and a hard-working athlete. But by Kelvin's junior year in high school, his attendance started slipping," Mrs. Wesley explained. "It was heartbreaking. He was being considered for a full scholarship to a major university. Scouts had watched him run and wanted him on their team." She explained that he had gotten into the wrong crowd and experimented with drugs. After that, he was not himself.

Mrs. Wesley paused and shook her head. Her eyes seemed to focus on the wall behind me. "He never understood why he didn't have a father," she said quietly. "His father left me before Kelvin was born. He wanted nothing to do with his child." The words hung in the courtroom air, before she continued her account. Mrs. Wesley had attempted several interventions with the help of their pastor, but they could not convince Kelvin to get help.

Pretty soon Kelvin had been arrested for grand theft. He dropped out of school before graduation. He lost any hope of getting a college scholarship and began to engage in activities that led him into the criminal justice system.

Now, as the deputy escorted him into the courtroom, Kelvin grinned at me and nodded his head in greeting. I nodded in return.

"Judge," his public defender, Mitchka Bavandi, said, "I met with Mr. Wesley in the jail, and he is highly motivated to participate in the court." I listened to Mitchka advocate on her client's behalf. "Mr. Wesley stated that he had never had the benefit of any kind of mental health or drug treatment."

I introduced myself and explained the court to Kelvin. I noticed that he seemed unusually engaged in the court process. "Could you and your mother join Janis and me at the bench?" I asked. "I will need your assistance in helping the court understand your background." Kelvin and his mother approached the bench.

"Mrs. Wesley," I asked, "has your son ever been evaluated by a mental health professional?"

"Yes, Judge," she said. "Kelvin was Baker Acted several years ago, when he became unmanageable and was behaving strangely. The doctors kept him in the hospital for several days and then referred him to the Henderson Behavioral Health Center. He was diagnosed with schizo-affective disorder, but Kelvin never followed through with his appointments."[11]

I had a gut feeling that Mrs. Wesley was holding something back. I understand it can be difficult to talk about sensitive family matters, but if Kelvin was going to participate in the court, I needed to understand his issues and areas of risk.

"Do you ever have any concerns about your safety or the safety of the other children in the house?" I asked.

Mrs. Wesley looked uncomfortable. Later, I would learn that she had not told Janis in their meeting that at times Kelvin acted out in anger.

"Judge, I generally have no problem with Kelvin. He is a good son," she said, choosing her words carefully. "But when he does drugs, he gets angry and I lock myself in the bedroom. I would say that he can, at times, have an anger problem."

Perhaps because of the look on my face, or her wanting to soften the blow of the news that her son could be violent enough that he scared her, but she added in a quiet voice, "He never had a father."

I calmly asked Janis to come to the side of the bench. I felt a need to talk to her discreetly. I wanted to work with him in the court, but his criminal history was serious and his anger issues raised concerns about risk. After a brief discussion, Janis suggested that we give him a chance. However, she was also concerned about his anger and the potential risk to his mother and other family members in the home. She recommended a residential program that offered treatment for mental health and substance use disorders. "If he is willing," Janis added.

As I discussed Janis's recommendations with Kelvin, he balked. He wanted to resolve his case and return home. I explained to him that the court was voluntary and this was the treatment plan that the court clinician believed that he needed. I explained to him that it was his choice. He did not have to participate in the court. If that was his choice, I would transfer his case back to the assigned division.

After much discussion with his public defender, Kelvin was still vacillating.

"Mr. Wesley," I said, "the choice is yours. I would only suggest that if you need mental health and drug treatment, you should get it. The research is well settled that untreated mental illness leads to several negative consequences, including addiction and incarceration. You are already being impacted by untreated mental health problems. Perhaps it's time you take a therapeutic approach and change your life. You deserve a healthy life. I heard you are a great athlete."

I never expected Kelvin to agree with me. He seemed confident in his position that he did not need help. To my surprise, however he said, "You know, Judge, no one has ever said that to me before. I want to try."

"That is a great choice," I said. "May I call you Kelvin? It's going to take a few days or so to secure a bed for you. Are you OK with that?"

"I am, Your Honor," he replied. "I want to go back to school and start running track again."

Mrs. Wesley, overcome with relief that perhaps there was hope, began to sob.

Within a few days, a bed became available. Kelvin appeared at the status hearing and we reviewed the order for his conditional release. He had agreed to successfully participate in the residential treatment program and abstain from any alcohol, intoxicants, or drugs. He would follow his mental health treatment plan. I explained to him that if any problems arose, to please tell the staff, who would request an immediate court hearing to review, and possibly change, the plan. I instructed Kelvin that he could not leave the program without court permission. Kelvin stated that he understood and agreed. The court staff was proud of his choice, particularly Mitchka, his public defender, who believed in him and patiently listened as he processed his decision whether to engage in care.

Less than twenty-four hours later, I received a text from JoAnne, my judicial assistant.

The clinical director of the program reported that at 9:00 p.m., Kelvin had jumped over the fence and absconded from the program.

I couldn't believe it.

In shock, I realized that he had not stayed at the facility for one day. I issued a writ for his arrest for violation of the conditional release order. Someone had to call his mother. Janis volunteered, since she had spent the most time with her and had the counseling skills to soften the blow.

At the next court hearing, there was no word of Kelvin and his whereabouts.

There was, however, positive news about Derrick. Janis reported that Ansom Phillips had phoned her to tell her that the Agency for Persons with Disabilities had identified a behavioral program for Derrick. It was in a rural part of Florida, where there was green space for Derrick to get out and enjoy recreation. Mr. Phillips and Dr. Kelly had reviewed the program and agreed that it was appropriate to meet Derrick's behavioral needs. Also, they felt that Derrick would be less likely to run away in a rural area.

A court hearing was convened, and we shared the news with Derrick. Like all of us, he was pleased that he would be leaving the jail system, but he wondered why his father had not visited him or come to court. Dr. Kelly explained to him that his father was doing the best he could to get settled and adjust to his new life outside prison, and that Derrick needed to do the same.

As the court continued follow Derrick's progress in the new program, we were delighted that, so far, he had not run away and seemed to be engaged in care. The reports included that he had developed a passion for basketball and had made progress in other functional areas. The court staff expressed relief that he was safe, had remained at the program, and had not been re-arrested. We considered this new program a significant and transformative shift in Derrick's life.

After I left the courthouse that afternoon, I drove toward downtown Fort Lauderdale to run a personal errand. As I stopped at a light at a busy intersection, I happened to glance to the left, and I spotted Kelvin. He was standing on a corner waiting to cross the street. He appeared clean and was dressed in fresh clothes, which made me think that perhaps he had returned home to his family. I didn't know what to do. Part of me wanted to lower my window and ask him why he left the program. I wanted to know why he was intent on ruining his life.

Instead, I immediately turned my head away to avoid eye contact with him. I wasn't sure that he would have recognized me, but I didn't want to take a chance. I couldn't predict what he would do if he did recognize me. I remembered how his mother had explained that he was "sometimes angry"—so much so that she locked herself in her bedroom in her own home. Kelvin had always appeared so calm and put together in court. Yet there was another side to him that I was sure I didn't want to see.

I thought about the people who had participated in the court whom we have helped, so many people. And yet, we cannot help everyone. Sometimes life experiences, trauma, and neglect become such large barriers that there aren't programs available to treat the years of broken thoughts and hearts. Kelvin, though, was young. He had so many strengths that he could have activated had he given the program a chance.

Four months later, Len Swadlow, the prosecutor in mental health court, informed me that Kelvin Wesley had been arrested, this time on felony charges for the sale and distribution of narcotics. I thought about his mother, how relieved she had been when she thought that help had finally arrived. In that moment she believed that her son, the track star, was going to be OK.

CHAPTER 14

A Referendum on Hope

It was a rainy Saturday morning as I sat in traffic on my way to the grocery store. My kids and I were doing our weekend errands: a stop at the dry cleaner, a swing through McDonald's for a pancake breakfast, and then to the grocery store. As the windshield wiper swooshed away the streaks of rain, I saw a woman standing on the side of the road, arguing with a police officer. Something about the argument drew my attention. I watched, transfixed by the strange scene. As I studied the woman, I realized that there was something familiar about her. I had seen her before. I pulled my car into the first parking lot near the dry cleaner to study her profile.

"What's going on?" my son asked.

"Hold on," I answered.

The argument between the officer and the woman continued. Something in our direction caught her eye, and she turned to face me. A jolt of shock ricocheted through my body. I recognized the face. She had been in mental health court. As raindrops slid down the window, the memories returned one by one: A courtroom scene. The Cottages. A national mental health conference in Miami. That way of speaking, gesturing richly with her hands.

It was Rosemarie.

Rosemarie had been a star. I remembered her on the stage of a national mental health conference years ago, when the court was still somewhat new, fielding questions from the audience in a style that modeled a TED talk. The ballroom of the downtown Miami hotel had been standing room only due to the number of mental health and criminal justice stakeholders who were eager to hear about her experience in the mental health court. The Broward County Mental Health Court was still in its infancy, but Congress had recently passed legislation to pilot mental health courts in other states across the nation.[1] Broward County's leap of faith to do something to take a stand against the criminalization of people with mental illness had surpassed our wildest dreams. When I was asked to lead the court, my immediate thought was "At least the court will treat the people it serves with dignity and respect." The conveyance of dignity is so fundamental to the court process that even if all else failed, at least the people the court served would know they had been respected, treated with dignity, and cared for. Fortunately, the shared vision of the community mental health and substance treatment providers empowered the court to succeed. Within a year, the court had diverted an estimated one thousand people from Broward's jail system, and this became an annual figure.

In 1999, I was sitting at my desk when an aide to Congressman Ted Strickland of Ohio called. She explained that Congressman Strickland, who had been following the court, wanted to introduce legislation to expand mental health courts nationally. She asked whether I would be willing to support such legislation. She indicated that staff had been researching the four mental health court models that were currently in existence—Broward County, Seattle, Anchorage, and San Bernardino—and wanted to propose a national demonstration project. I offered my support.

Congressman Strickland filed a bill in the House in 1999, and Senator Mike DeWine, also of Ohio, filed a companion bill in the Senate in the same year. Over the next year, I engaged in a national campaign to support mental health courts and CIT (crisis intervention training) diversionary strategies, along with Major Sam Cochran (ret.) of the Memphis Police Department.

On November 13, 2000, President Bill Clinton signed the legislation into law, and mental health courts became a reality not for just four, but for many more communities.[2]

Rosemarie had been so happy for the chance to tell her story to the conference attendees—how she had suffered from untreated mental illness and how the court had found her housing and treatment services at the Cottages. She had spoken vibrantly, proudly, about the friendships she formed with other residents and about the strides she had made in her own life. "I'm living my life in a way I never thought I could. I want to have a part-time job, and I want to start taking classes at the local community college. I love to garden and read. I couldn't be happier," she had told the conference, beaming.

I couldn't recall the last time I had seen Rosemarie. She had lived at the Cottages in the Pines for just over a year. She had formed close friendships with two other residents, Margaret and Sharon, who interviewed her frequently for the newsletter they had started there. And Rosemarie had joined me on stage that day at the conference. It had been an exuberant experience to share the stage with her—one I'll always remember.

As Rosemarie's participation in mental health court wound down, her case was closed. As the years passed, I lost track of her as she moved on from the Cottages and forward with her life.

There really is no way to keep track of the thousands of people—more than twenty thousand—who have been participants in the mental health court. Some have worked with the court longer than others, depending on the complexity of their treatment and social service needs and issues of risk and legal competency. My hope is that people who continue to make their mental health a priority will apply the many lessons learned about recovery, wellness, and the need to champion mental health in their families. It is OK that they move on with their lives. In fact, they are supposed to; that means the court is working. But some court participants fell by the wayside, and either we never found out about it, or we found out by accident—as with Rosemarie.

———————————

"Stay in the car!" I said to my kids in the backseat. They looked at me with confused expressions but nodded. Then, I stepped out of the car and walked over to the sidewalk where the heated exchange was occurring.

The legal voice in my head was screaming, *Do not get arrested for interfering with the execution of a police investigation!* I walked very slowly toward Rosemarie and the police officer. I made sure I stayed far enough away so as not to interfere. I barely recognized Rosemarie. *This was not possible*, I thought. The star of the Cottages who had presented to hundreds of people at a national mental health conference in crisp, professional attire now had an orange lightning bolt painted on each side of her face. She was filthy, and her wet clothing was tattered and hung heavily around her body. On feet that had once worn stylish high heels, she now had tied the tops of shoe boxes in place of shoes. Nothing about her was recognizable aside from some hint of the person I'd come to know in mental health court. Her words tripped over each other incoherently as she flung them at the officer in nonsensical waves. He continued to ask her what she was trying to say, and she spoke ever more rapidly. She was becoming highly agitated.

How did this happen? She was doing so well!

I stood in silence and observed the scene. The police officer, a very large man, loomed over her. As I approached, his tone changed, and he began to yell at Rosemarie, "Get in my car!"

Rosemarie appeared not to understand his commands. She flung frenzied sounds at the officer, waving her arms wildly. The longer she stood there in the rain, the more aggravated the police officer became. The encounter was so intense that the police officer never turned to acknowledge my presence.

"Excuse me, sir," I said. "I'm Judge Lerner-Wren. I'm a mental health court judge, and this woman is in my court." His eyes were so angry I thought they were burning holes through me, despite the cold rain. I wondered if I had made a mistake by interfering, but there was no going back now. So I continued: "I wanted to let you know that she is intellectually disabled and suffers from schizophrenia. . . . So, I . . . I thought this information might help you."

The police officer grew more angry and his face turned beet red. He looked me straight in the eye and snapped, "If you want her, *you* take her!"

Then the officer, beyond exasperated, took advantage of the exit strategy I'd unintentionally presented him with, jumped into his police cruiser, and sped away. The police car disappeared in the traffic, leaving me alone with Rosemarie in the rain.

I returned my gaze to Rosemarie. For a moment, her eyes met mine and flickered. I studied her face. This was not the person I had known. I tried to recall how long it had been since she was at the Cottages and participating in the court. Was it five, seven, or ten years? How long does it take for a life to go sideways?

Up close, she looked frightening. The orange lightning bolts painted on her cheeks accentuated the wild, feral look of her entire body. I did not want her to be hurt or arrested, but I certainly had not expected this to happen. I had hoped the police officer would help me contact the mobile crisis team, who had the skills to de-escalate the situation. It was clear Rosemarie needed help, but I was certainly not capable of providing the kind of help she needed in this precise moment. The rain fell on both of us, each one afraid to move, for our own separate reasons.

This had turned into a nightmare.

Rosemarie broke the standstill moment first, assuming a posture that may have been what caught the police officer's attention. "Give me money, give me money!" she demanded in a deep voice that was unfamiliar to me.

I took a step back from her, suddenly afraid. I felt for the familiar bag around my shoulder and realized I didn't have my purse. I had left it in the car, with the kids.

Alone on a long stretch of sidewalk in the rain, I didn't know what to do. At this point, Rosemarie's psychosis prevented me from engaging her in any kind of conversation. She was getting more aggressive. I didn't attempt to reason with her because I didn't believe she had the ability to understand me. The only thing I could do was try to appease her. "OK," I said, "I'll get you money. But you have to wait here."

The car was parked a few yards away. I could see the faces of my son and daughter in the backseat peering out the rear window.

In calm voice, I explained to Rosemarie that I needed to walk past her to get my purse. I also needed to call Henderson's mobile crisis team, but I felt that I should make sure the kids were safe before I did anything.

Rosemarie allowed me to walk to the car, but did not heed my direction to wait on the sidewalk as I retrieved my purse. Instead, she followed a couple of paces behind me. I began to sweat as I approached my car door, hoping she would not force her way in.

I motioned to the kids to sit still and stay quiet. I did not want to escalate an already tense situation. I opened the car door and saw a box of cereal that one of the kids had brought. I picked it up and handed it to Rosemarie, thinking she was hungry and that having something to eat would distract her until I found my wallet.

I reached inside the car for my purse, grabbed a few dollar bills from my wallet, and quickly handed them to Rosemarie. "Here, why don't you go to the store at the gas station and get some coffee or something to drink with your cereal," I said as I pointed to the gas station on the corner.

Rosemarie took the money and began to walk in the opposite direction, toward the gas station.

I got into the car and breathed deeply. I realized I was shaking. I called Henderson and asked for the mobile crisis team to come to the gas station. Then I tried to reach Rosemarie's former community case manager. I began to realize that I was soaked from standing in the rain for so long. The sound of the world, which had gone silent, returned: the swoosh of passing cars, the click of tires moving across the road, the distant discord of a car alarm.

I tried to process what had just happened. It was surreal. How could this woman, who had been such a stellar success, have fallen so far?

It was heartbreaking. I put my hands on the steering wheel and could not hold back my tears. I put the car in drive and slowly pointed us in the direction of the grocery store, our remaining errand. I held my breath as I silently cried. I cared about Rosemarie.

What I had witnessed was a tragedy. I had no idea what was going to happen to her. And although I had given her money, something to eat, and had called the crisis team, I had a sinking feeling. She had been to the mental health court years before and that hadn't led to a healthier life. *Was there nothing I could do to help her?*

I had failed to note the name of the police officer who confronted Rosemarie that day. I did not blame him for his heavy-handed behavior. Everything had happened so fast. I speculated that he had worked all night or may have been under stress about something that had nothing to do with Rosemarie's behavior. My friends and colleagues whom I told about the encounter were critical of my decision to intervene. "What were you thinking, Ginger? What if the police officer thought that you were trying to hinder his investigation— even if you believed you trying to help?" they asked.

I did not have a good answer, other than I felt that the officer needed to know that the woman who had rankled him was mentally ill and needed help. I feared that she might be harmed.

If the officer had been specially trained in responding to crisis and the detection and de-escalation of people with mental illness, perhaps the encounter would have gone better. I was more interested, however, in what had happened to Rosemarie since I last saw her. How had the system failed her when she left the Cottages? Clearly, she had not been properly transitioned to permanent housing or provided with the means to access the proper services. Given her strengths and her abilities, she could have lived independently with supports. She might have become interested in taking a part-time job or become engaged in mental health advocacy and peer support activities.

All that investment in her mental health treatment and care for so many years, had it been for naught? This is the great unknown. What will happen to court participants once their case is over? Recovery is defined as "a process of change through which individuals improve their health and wellness, live a self-directed life, and strive to reach their full potential."[3] What is essential is to understand that recovery isn't a single occurrence. It is a process, one that requires consistency and attention. It is important to remember that recovery is hardly ever sequential or linear. Furthermore, each person's journey to recovery is unique. Sometimes, as in the case of Rosemarie, there can be frightening setbacks.

Yet, for people with strong support networks of family and friends, there are safety nets that prevent a mental illness from taking a person down too far. Without that safety net, however, there is absolutely nothing to keep a person's life from slipping away, one moment at a time. It is heartbreaking to consider that Rosemarie fell through the cracks of a highly fragmented and underfunded system of mental health care to find herself in an ongoing nightmare where relationships, health, memories, and even her sense of self fade.

Philip Reynaldo was fifty-two years old and homeless. He liked to hang around the Fort Lauderdale bus station, which is where many of the city's homeless population congregate. Fort Lauderdale, like all major US cities, has a significant number of homeless people. Without access to affordable housing and jobs, most people are not able to get off the streets, even though there are several homeless shelters sprinkled throughout the county. Without housing resources, there is no effective way to move people off the streets. Instead, people continue to cycle in and out of jail, shelters, and hospital emergency rooms.

Philip was a frequent participant in the court. He had never connected to mental health care, although the court staff always was intent on ensuring that he did not languish in jail and that he received acute psychiatric care, treatment, and stabilization at the nearest Baker Act receiving facility. His arrests were always for minor nuisances and quality-of-life offenses such as panhandling or urinating in public. He was a fixture in the court system.

Philip was an intensive and frequent user of local services, with no end in sight. I was serious when I said, "It would be cheaper for Broward County to pay to house him."

Until one day, when we found it: a solution.

"Mr. Reynaldo," I asked when he returned to court from the Fort Lauderdale Hospital, "how are you doing?"

"I feel good, Judge. Thank you."

"You know, Philip," I said, "all of the court staff marvel at how well you do on your medication. We were thinking that perhaps this time, you may be interested in working with the court so we can help you break these cycles of arrest. They cannot be good for you. And you have so much to offer."

My sentiments were genuine. Even though we had gotten to know Philip, we still didn't know much about his personal history except that he had suffered a traumatic brain injury from a car accident. We also knew that when he took his medication, his mood, demeanor, and capacity to make sound decisions improved considerably. He became a kind, witty, and personable man.

Surprisingly, Philip said he would like to try working with the court. I smiled, hoping that this would be the decision that would change his life for the better.

"I'm so glad you do," I said.

Philip appeared at his review hearings for several months, as we monitored how he was doing and whether he required additional services. His progress was remarkable. He began to transform before our eyes. Who knew that he had a keen interest in men's fashion? One day he appeared in court dressed in dark blue jeans and a red, white, and black striped shirt. He topped his look off with a black-tweed newsboy cap. It was impressive.

Within weeks, however, Philip was back in jail. He had been arrested for panhandling. The next time I saw him in court he was wearing a loose-fitting jail jumpsuit. He had stopped taking his medication and needed to be transported to the hospital for psychiatric treatment and stabilization. He had returned to his former life, to the streets.

It was heartbreaking.

When Philip returned to court again following his discharge from the Fort Lauderdale Hospital, I asked him what had happened to get him back to this point again. He had been doing so well.

He lifted his shoulders in an exasperated shrug. He had no answer. In a gesture of goodwill and to preserve his dignity, I suggested to him that perhaps he simply did not have enough positive support to pivot to a new life.

"Perhaps," I said, "your friends who were homeless did not want you to leave them."

I thought about Rosemarie and wondered whether her homelessness was by choice or whether the struggle for a new life was just too challenging without the support she had enjoyed at the Cottages.

Philip shrugged again. Like the rest of us, he just didn't have an answer.

After years of serving on its bench, however, I did. For me, the greatest failing of the court stems from my idealism. I was confident that as media attention grew, so would the public's outcry against what Ron Honberg, the senior policy adviser for the National Alliance on Mental Illness, and members of other mental health policy organizations labeled the "inappropriate criminalization of people with mental illness."[4] Clearly, serious crime warrants punishment. Yet I believed that when minor criminal acts were viewed through the therapeutic justice lens of a court of dignity, that the shame of injustice would be evident.

It wasn't—not yet.

As these stories reveal, the vast majority of people who have participated in the court have never seen a mental health practitioner. In many cases their families knew "something was wrong," but could not identify the problem as a serious mental health disorder. Or, when a mental health crisis occurred, individuals and families had no health insurance and could not navigate systems of care that are highly fragmented and underfunded. Further, disparities based upon race, ethnicity, class, and education make up the lion's share of the justice-involved population. People who suffer from these disparities encounter barriers to care with regards to stigma and a mistrust of the mental health system that must be appreciated to understand how to enhance engagement in mental health care. These barriers to care are particularly challenging when hope for jail diversion and precise treatment matching is reliant on access to publicly funded community resources. Resources such as supported housing programs and an array of residential treatment programs, like affordable housing and residential treatment programs, are very limited if they are available at all.

The barriers to care surrounding mental illness are such that fourteen years ago, the New Freedom Commission on Mental Health determined that nothing short of system transformation would remediate the problems and achieve the mission that President George W. Bush outlined in his executive order establishing the commission in 2002.[5] The president's goal was to establish a mental-health-care delivery system in the United States that enables adults with serious mental illness and children with serious emotional disturbances to live, work, learn, and fully participate in their communities. This goal has not yet been achieved.

According to research, one in five Americans, 43.8 million people, experience mental illness in a given year. Despite the prevalence of mental illness, research conducted by the National Institute of Mental Health has found that nearly 60 percent of adults and 50 percent of youth who had such an episode in the year previous to the study did not receive mental health services.[6] The consequences of untreated mental illness are profound and costly in human, social, and economic terms. Even with the proliferation of problem-solving mental health and other treatment courts, an estimated four hundred thousand people incarcerated in America's jails and prisons.[7]

Combating this trend, the Broward County Mental Health Court and other mental health courts provide valuable lessons and insights into recovery and the power of community, human connections, and ways to leverage social networks and alliances to provide supports to fill gaps. These bold efforts, however, also highlight the need for our nation's policymakers to "turn the page" of centuries of stigma and discrimination and advance mental health reforms from a public health perspective—as opposed to a criminal justice perspective—as urged by many national experts, including Arthur C. Evans Jr., the chief executive officer of the American Psychological Association. According to Dr. Evans, "Mental health requires a public health approach, which is more like treating diabetes than a broken leg." A rational mental health or behavioral health delivery system must be informed about the diverse needs of their communities and as stated by Dr. Evans, "develop strategies to prevent, treat, and rehabilitate individuals with varied and diverse problems including serious mental illness and substance use."[8]

Make no mistake: I enthusiastically support problem-solving courts and work to promote the principles and application of therapeutic jurisprudence in all legal spheres. The goals of problem-solving justice and community restorative justice approaches, in my view, are the future of our legal system. But there is one caveat.

These court strategies, which look to respond to root causes and the vexing social problems that land on the courthouse steps, are not and were never intended to be a substitute for a comprehensive public health model of mental-health and behavioral-health care in the United States. There is a great deal of work to do from a public health perspective to transform mental-health and behavioral-health care delivery for all Americans. After all, mental health is essential to overall health.

On July 22, 2002, the New Freedom Commission on Mental Health submitted its final report to the White House.[9] In a cover letter drafted by the commission chair, Michael F. Hogan, the commission was pleased to report that after a year of extensive study and review of the research and testimony, the commission had concluded that "recovery from mental illness is now a real possibility. The promise of the New Freedom Initiative—a life in the community for everyone—can be realized. But only if the nation undergoes a fundamental transformation in its approach to healthcare."[10]

In August 2008, Janis Blenden, the in-court clinician, and I were invited to present on the Broward County Mental Health Court at the International Conference on Special Needs Offenders, convened by the International Institute on Special Needs and Policy Research, in Niagara Falls, Canada. The conference focus was on mentally ill offenders and special populations including women, indigenous people, and residents of underdeveloped countries. Conference attendees included four large and diverse delegations of criminal justice and mental health stakeholders from Canada, the United States, the United Kingdom, and Kenya. Although we had not been informed that our session was of particular interest to the delegation members from Kenya, that fact became clear to me as I had an opportunity to sit next to Dr. Manford Meli, a mental health policy consultant, who led the delegation.

In many countries, a lack of rational and comprehensive mental health policies serves to perpetuate stigma and discrimination of those living with mental illness. The World Health Organization has reported that 40 percent of countries do not have a mental health policy, and 25 percent of countries do not have mental health legislation or a rational national mental health agenda.[11] The Broward County Mental Health Court, which was established without government funding or grants, offers a cost-effective, sustainable, innovative strategy for other countries to consider, especially if they are interested in transitioning to a more humane, community-centered approach to mental health care.

Over lunch, Dr. Meli explained that he had accepted an assignment to participate in the development of comprehensive mental health agenda on behalf of the government of Kenya. He described an array of challenges that intersected with every domain of public health infrastructure in Kenya. These challenges included establishing legislative and disability rights law and social justice policies to mitigate health inequities and to begin to close existing gaps in mental health care. There was no system of mental health care at all in Kenya. Instead, there was only one state hospital to serve the entire nation; the hospital was essentially an overcrowded prison. The inhumane conditions at Mathari Hospital in Nairobi gained international attention for the need for national reform in 2013, when forty patients escaped. The subsequent reporting revealed several shortcomings of Kenya's budget; mental health care was funded at less than 1 percent of the annual budget.[12]

As my lunch conversation with Dr. Meli ended, I realized that the delegation from Kenya may have come to the conference for information, but what they needed was hope.

As the first speaker took the podium to open the presentation about mental health courts, instead of providing a historical context for the development of this problem-solving court model in the United States, he opened his presentation with comments showing what clearly was intended to express his disapproval of the mental health court model, as he sternly stated, "There is no evidence or data that mental health courts work." I did not take the speaker's comment seriously in terms of his presentation of data. I knew that mental health courts, which use a dignity model, are highly effective, as research on Broward County's Mental Health Court has clearly demonstrated.

According to Michael L. Perlin, advocates should seize on the ratification of the UN's Convention on the Rights of Persons with Disabilities (CRPD) to push through the expansion of mental health courts to create an international movement on behalf of persons with mental disabilities. He notes, "Individuals with mental disabilities have been outsiders in the world of international human rights law, with many important global human rights agencies traditionally expressing little to no interest in the plight of this cohort."[13] Perlin argues that with the ratification of the CRPD and with the model of Broward County Mental Health Court and other mental health courts, judges who apply the principles of therapeutic jurisprudence dignity can remediate the inhumane treatment of prisoners with mental illness.[14]

Perlin states, "The Convention is the most revolutionary international human rights document ever created that applies to persons with disabilities."[15] I concur with his view that mental health courts that promote dignity have the capacity to mitigate the inhumane treatment of persons with mental disabilities. Dignity is the leading objective of the Broward County Mental Health Court, to redress a number of factors: centuries of false and irrational attitudes surrounding mental illness, institutional bias and stigma against people with mental disabilities, the tragic experiences of Aaron Wynn, and the highly fragmented and under-resourced community-based system of mental health care. From working in the South Florida State Hospital and as a public guardian, I have witnessed firsthand the marginalization and degradation of my clients. This experience led me to create a court culture of dignity and respect. The application of therapeutic jurisprudence and the aspirational goals of the UN Convention give the court impetus to protect individuals' constitutional and due process rights and promote human connectedness and trust by providing defendants a voice, validation, and voluntariness.

This example of human connection enhances the perception of fairness, levels the playing field, and instills hope. This is the profound message of the mental health court, nationally and internationally. As noted in a recent publication that surveyed hundreds of mental health courts in the United States and Australia, "The Broward County MHC's influence on international practice is manifest. In Australia, jail has not been used as a sanction in any its four MHCs."[16] According to Michelle Edgely, mental health courts are gaining in popularity in the United States and internationally, with more than four hundred mental health courts in the United States and around the world. With a focus on what makes a mental health court work, Edgely examines a number of theoretical aspects of judicial approaches in a problem-solving court and argues that the most effective approach in a mental health court to promote rehabilitation pertains to "building therapeutic alliances."[17] Although Edgely notes that more research is needed to evaluate the effectiveness of mental health courts work as to recidivism and rehabilitation, she notes that "a significant body" of data as to mental health court outcomes both in the United States and Australia provide evidence that these courts are effective at reducing recidivism.[18]

My awareness of recent evidence of the effectiveness of mental health courts didn't prevent me, as I paced up and down the side of the conference room as the first speaker shared his views, from being concerned about the impact of the speaker's remarks on the audience. Many who had come to this session seeking inspiration and a robust exchange of ideas on how to advocate for social change in underdeveloped regions.

How do you generate hope?

That first speaker may well have dashed the Kenya delegation's perception of finding a solution at the conference within a matter of minutes. I glanced at Dr. Meli. His head was down, and as I scanned the room, I noticed that the audience members were looking at me with doubt. I thought about the desperation of Broward County and the release of the scathing 1994 Broward County grand jury report.[19] Of course, data is critically important to guide mental health policy and budget decisions. In the report, Broward County's inadequate mental health community-based system of care had been adjudged "deplorable." At times, innovation emerges from desperation, and Broward's Mental Health Court was an example of an innovation that grew out of the need to "do something."

I felt that the members of the Kenya delegation needed to understand the power of hope and that they shouldn't be deterred to bring their own justice innovations forward, as social justice is a matter of life and death. I got up from the speakers' table where Janis and I were sitting and began to pace up and down the side of the conference breakout room. I thought about a moment fifteen years before when a chief judge at a criminal justice forum suggested that what I was doing in the Broward County Mental Health Court was "wholly inappropriate." I remember how hard that comment struck me. For me, as a new judge, those words had delivered a hefty load of doubt. How was I going to restore hope to the members of the delegation? As I waited for the opportunity to deliver my rebuttal, I thought about hope and its inextricable connection to vision.

I began my speech with the words "Data schmata." This was not a comment about the importance of data and the need to develop outcome measures or an evidence base of "what works." It was, instead, my way of reinvigorating hope. I meant it as a reminder that there is a time for action and leadership, particularly when there are vacuums in social policy that impact basic human rights and health, and the need for more data should not become an obstacle to such action. It was my referendum on hope.

As I spoke, I described the problems that the Broward County community had been experiencing in the criminal justice system when a small group of stakeholders decided to create a task force to search for solutions to the overrepresentation of people arrested with mental health and cognitive disorders in our local jail system. I explained that the mental health court was born out of desperation and as a response to suffering and human rights violations, and I described the transformative case of Aaron Wynn. The court was the physical manifestation of a community's collective hope that they could find a solution—something—that worked.

"The court was our 'something,'" I said.

The room burst out with applause that was so loud, conference officials who hadn't heard applause that loud before rushed into the room to see if something was wrong.

Broward County's mental health system has never recovered from the financial crisis of 2008 and the decision by the Department of Children and Families to accelerate privatization of the behavioral-health-care system, which occurred several years after the conference. Its result was a notable decrease in the number of mental health services and treatment programs available not only to citizens of Broward County but to the state of Florida. Even as the mental health court continues to adapt to ever-changing mental health policy while working to address the needs of the community, each new challenge leads me back to the speech I gave years before in Canada. As of 2017, the community-based system of mental health care hadn't yet expanded its service capacity for mental health care, residential care, and housing. Then, as now, I wonder: How will the court fill gaps and limitations in Broward's community-based mental health care?

And how were we going to restore hope, not only for the court, but for me?

CHAPTER 15

Recovery Is Real

The story of Kathryn Steeves's descent into homelessness and mental illness—and her journey back to health—tells a larger story than many might give her credit for. It is a story about loss, certainly; but it is also a story about the strength of human character and our ability to overcome insurmountable odds. Kathryn, middle-aged, watched her marriage fall apart and life with her children become more stressful.

So, one night she simply walked away, closing and locking the door behind her—a final closure on the life she had once loved. Walking into the darkened street, Kathryn abandoned her life for what she might have thought was forever. And yet, it wasn't forever.

The lessons and insights that Kathryn and others have learned about the need for comprehensive care and person-centered psychiatric rehabilitation are relevant, but more important, they are real. The welcoming by a compassionate and supportive system of mental health care is essential for people with mental illness to become resilient, achieve recovery, and live a self-directed life in the community. Because, in the end, recovery isn't an illusion. Recovery is a part of the human condition and the story of each of our lives.

When I met Kathryn, her dream was to be reunited with her children. She came to the mental health court after two years of living homeless on the street, a condition prompted by a case of undiagnosed and consequently untreated bipolar disorder that was triggered by the stress of her dissolving marriage. Then her children were taken from her. Filled with despair, Kathryn decided that if she did not have her children, then she did not need her home. She told me that she realized she had lost everything the moment she appeared in mental health court. Somehow she had survived for over two years, without friends, family, reliable shelter, or any means of support.

The mental health court connected her to a residential treatment service called the Cottages in the Pines. When she arrived, she was introduced to a young and ambitious community case manager, Magadalia Perez, a self-described "fireball." Kathryn credits Magadalia "with saving her life."

Kathryn lived at the Cottages for nearly one year, when she learned that it was time for her to prepare to leave the program. Kathryn was anxious and excited about her chance to start over. Now more in touch with her feelings after intensive therapeutic work, Kathryn wanted to set herself goals that aligned with her mission in life. When the time came to put pen to paper Magadalia asked Kathryn, "What do you want to be?"

Kathryn smiled and said, "I want to be you."

Kathryn applied to college and was accepted to a degree program in mental health counseling. Then, with Magadalia's support, she petitioned the family court judge to grant her custody of her children.

The petition was granted, and Kathryn's long and arduous journey back to her children was over.

After twenty years, I've come to appreciate that anything can happen on a Thursday. Thursday dockets were always rigorous. The diverse mix of cases includes people who have been discharged from the hospital, new court referrals, and cases that have been continued from the session the day before because the problem-solving re-quired by each case was complex and required more time to negoti-ate systems and to coordinate care.

As I listened to Janis update the status of a defendant, a woman with blond hair entered the courtroom. The court deputy who mon-itored the door politely stopped her to inquire if she had a matter on the docket. As they spoke, a nagging sense that there was some-thing familiar about her tugged at me. My mind flipped through the years as though they were index cards, flickering through court-room scenes and life stories. After she finished speaking with the court deputy, she turned toward me.

As I looked at her face, I recognized her. She stood where she had stood years before, when she had been a participant in the mental health court.

Lilly. How could I ever forget Lilly?

The power struggle between us had been extraordinary. If I only had a video playback of those hearings, where I was virtually plead-ing with her to let us help her. Lilly, like Kathryn, had been home-less. Unlike Kathryn, she had been unable to fully comprehend that her ex-husband had obtained a restraining order against her: Lilly was prohibited from returning to the family home or having contact with her children, even though she did return to the family home and did have contact with her children several times before her case was referred to the mental health court. Each time, I thought—hoped—that she would agree to the court's offers of assistance. Instead, she would raise new obstacles to what had already been negotiated.

Yet here she was. I hadn't seen her for more than a decade. But the way she glided as she traversed the courtroom had not changed.

As she approached the bench, I could see her more clearly. She had aged. But then, so had I.

"Lilly," I said. "Goodness! What brings you here? Is everything all right?"

"Everything is fine," she said. "I just wanted to say hello."

I felt like I had just been transported back in time. Everything seemed so familiar. Lilly was wearing a black and white flowing, bohemian dress with a sheer white shawl draped over her shoulders.

Her blond hair was piled in a neat bun on top of her head. I was glad that she had not changed her style in all those years. It suited her too well.

"Allen," I said to my deputy clerk, "I am going to take a brief recess."

I escorted Lilly into the jury room to talk. We sat directly across from each other. "It is wonderful to see you," I said. "What brings you to court?"

"I wanted to come and thank you," she said. "If it were not for you and the court, I don't think I would be where I am in my life today. Actually, I'm not even sure I would be *here*."

She told me that she resided in a "delightful" assisted-living facility near the beach. "I spend time with my children. We're close," she said. Then she paused, taking a breath before saying with pride, "And can you believe it? I'm a grandmother." She told me that one of her daughters lived in Thailand but telephones often.

She told me about her hobbies—her plants and her garden— and how the white gardenia plant blooms on her private patio and its rich and sweet aroma. She told me about the bougainvillea plant that grew and twined around her living room window. She told me about watching sunrises and sunsets over the ocean, which was not far from her home. The ocean, she said, was big, but even so, it was unchanging and constant. That, she said, was a comfort.

"I wanted you to know that I'm happy," she said. We sat for a few minutes and spoke like two old friends who had known each other in another time.

Then I told her about my life, or the court's life. "The court is being considered for a prestigious award in the Netherlands," I said.

Lilly wished us luck.

As the visit wound down, we looked at each other in silence and smiled.

"Thank you for treating me so well," she said. "My mother always taught me to treat people as you would want to be treated. I just don't think I would be this far in my life if it wasn't for you."

Her words meant a great deal to me, particularly since we had sparred so much in the beginning of her case. Who can know the impact we have on the lives of others? This was a voice from the past, an unexpected "hello" when the path of Lilly's life crossed mine once again. I wondered, briefly, about the other lives with which mine had intersected as a result of my work in the mental health court. But as I gathered their names in my mind, I realized that there was really no way of knowing. Not unless they came to see me, as Lilly had done, or if by chance our paths crossed once again.

Kathryn has been a constant fixture in the mental health court since she earned her degree in mental health counseling and achieved her goal to serve others, as a mental health community case manager. Fifteen years after she first appeared in Broward's Mental Health Court, Kathryn and I once again worked together. Debbie Plotnick of Mental Health America invited me to participate in a webinar hosted by the Rosalynn Carter Fellowships for Mental Health Journalism.[1] Along with her invitation, she also asked me whether I knew of a Broward County Mental Health Court participant who would also be interested in being on the panel. I knew that instant that I had to call Kathryn.

I chose to do the webinar from my home as opposed to the courthouse because we needed quiet. There was no way to control the phones or the commotion in the corridor outside my chambers.

I set up desk chairs directly in front of the computer screen, with two headsets, and I hung talking points on the wall next to the computer, in case we needed reminders. Kathryn and I took our seats in front of the computer screen to wait for the Skype call.

The Rosalyn Carter Fellowship is highly competitive and attracts top journalists who have an interest in mental health. The goals of the fellowship are to increase accurate reporting on mental health issues, reduce stereotypical information, enhance the quality of the journalists reporting, and develop a network of informed professional journalists across the news, magazine, radio, film, television, and social media.

The topic of this webinar was mental health, decriminalization, and jail diversion. As the webinar began, I started the presentation by describing the problems that Broward County had experienced in its criminal justice system, which had led to the development of the mental health court. These problems included a lack of access to mental health treatment and services in the community, jail over-crowding, several deaths by suicide in the jail, and other failures outlined in the grand jury investigation of Broward County's mental health system.[2]

Debbie Plotnick discussed the criminalization of people with mental illness and co-occurring substance disorders, as well as the failed deinstitutionalization policies that have left thousands of people with serious mental illness with nowhere to go.[3] Katti Gray, the moderator, talked about community collaboration and then shifted the questioning to Kathryn.

"Can you describe your experience as a mental health consumer and the challenges that you and—now that you work in the field—your clients face?" Katti asked.

As Kathryn spoke, the webinar took on a deeper human focus. I am sure that the Rosalynn Carter fellows watching the webinar ap-preciated her perspective. On a personal level, I learned a great deal as I listened to Kathryn describe her experience in the court. She explained, "The court provided me with a pathway to transitional housing. That was a priority for me, since I was homeless. I doubt I would have been able to find housing for myself in the state that I was in back then."

Kathryn spoke from the heart and explained that the one of the greatest unmet social needs of her clients is housing. She stated that many of her clients reside in shoddy and unsanitary assisted-living facilities because they are dependent on Social Security dis-ability payments and can only afford this poor-quality housing. Af-ter paying for even that, many of the clients do not have any money left to buy clothes, food, or necessities. Forget about going to a movie or buying an occasional treat. The level of poverty that her clients endure was "shameful," Kathryn said. "I often feel guilty. I can't do more for the people I serve, even if they deserve more," she said.

As the webinar came to a close, the moderator went around the panel and asked each of us to share with the fellows what wish we would want to have granted for mental health and criminal justice. Without prior discussion, Kathryn and I interestingly expressed the same wish, but she articulated it more succinctly: "I wish that a new era of mental health would emerge where it was universally accepted that 'recovery is real.'" In her voice one heard the years of exasperation with the fact that this was not yet the case. Her voice carried deep pain, I realized, as I listened to Kathryn speak. But it also carried great passion.

When the moderator asked Kathryn why she decided on that wish, Kathryn replied, "I believe that access to qualitative, comprehensive mental health and substance abuse treatment should be available in our communities. People with mental health problems should not have to wait for crisis to get help." After a pause, she added, "People were made to get better. Our bodies and minds have adapted to facing challenges and learning about them, and then we can overcome them. Recovery is not a myth. Recovery is a reality."

Days after the interview, I attended a luncheon meeting at one of Broward County's leading civic organizations. At first, it was off to a positive start. The restaurant was elegant and had been closed to the public to accommodate the civic group. The organizer's plan was to have a "working lunch." The program was titled "Overcoming Stigma and Mental Health," which I thought was a great topic for a civic group. I was especially looking forward to getting a better understanding of the views of people who are not part of the mental health community.

The civic organization was diverse and included a mix of city officials, civic activists, and business leaders. Several panelists spoke eloquently about the impact of stigma from various perspectives. Unfortunately, by the time it was my turn to speak, most of the speakers had left after delivering their remarks.

Since I was the only speaker left, I felt I should stay for the Q&A session.

"Anyone have a question?" I asked. A man at the opposite end of the table nodded at me as he raised his hand.

"Yes, sir?" I said.

"Where do you put 'em?" He asked and leaned back in his chair.

"What do you mean? Where do I put what?" I asked.

"You know, the people that you see in your mental court," he said.

"I don't put them anywhere, sir," I said. "They are people."

I could feel the tension in the room growing. It was a derogatory comment, and several people looked confused. It was not so much what he said as how he said it, and I knew exactly what he intended to imply: his voice was cold and disdainful, as if he were asking where put excess plates in a kitchen cabinet that has run out of space.

I remained composed and proceeded to spend the next several minutes discussing the prevalence of mental illness, the fact that everyone's healthcare needs are different, and the reasons it is so important that policymakers at every level of government in Broward County prioritize mental health.

Then, another hand shot up.

"Judge, if Broward County spends more for mental health services, won't that attract more homeless people?" this man asked. "You know, our community has a serious homeless problem."

I responded to this man's question as best I could. It struck me that these views and attitudes about mental illness that were being expressed were more than likely how most people understood the issue of mental health. The perception that all people with mental illness are homeless is stereotypical and false. Yet this seems to be a common view. You don't need research to tell you that not all mentally ill are homeless. The fact that several homeless people also have untreated mental illnesses would indicate a lack of services and resources to connect those individuals with care. The solution, therefore, is not one based on the issue of homelessness but on the amount of mental health resources and services available to serve our communities. That is why I work hard in the court to reinforce the message that treatment works. And this is why I rely on health literacy and the promotion of dignity to help level the playing field. I have tried to create a stigma-free environment where people can envision their dreams. But a courtroom is just one small space.

I spent the last few minutes of the luncheon talking about recovery and humanizing the people I see in court. I hope I changed a few minds by the time the luncheon was over.

Over the years, I have often thought about Roger, whose case was the first to be heard by the Broward County Mental Health Court, and wondered how he was doing. The memory of the opening day of the court—how it rapidly turned into a traumatic event—is forever etched in my mind. It was a harrowing experience for me as the presiding judge to have to order the courtroom cleared because Roger was too psychiatrically unstable to understand what was happening. He was so agitated, I feared he would pull the chair in the jury box out of the floor. The court's first case led to its first order to divert a mental health defendant out of the jail, to be transported to a local receiving facility for psychiatric evaluation and treatment. I issued the order in the corridor outside the courtroom.

Once Roger was connected to mental health treatment and care in the community, his case was dismissed. We never saw or heard from him again. But I will never forget the way he smiled as he stood in the courtroom, reunited with his parents who had lost him to untreated mental illness and the streets. Since the court heard Roger's case, more than twenty thousand people have come through the Broward County Mental Health Court. We may not have been able to help everyone, but together with a mental health community collaborative, we have touched many lives.

It was a bright spring morning when I left my house to drive to the courthouse. I took the same route that I have taken every morning for nearly twenty years, passing the same homes, and watched as parents walked their children to the elementary school nearby. On this particular day, I noticed a tall man walking toward the bus stop. It was a bus stop that I had passed countless times before, and I had never seen anyone waiting at that bus stop. But this man stopped there to wait for the bus. There was something familiar about him.

It didn't take me long to piece it together—it was Roger. He looked different than I recalled, but there was no doubt that it was him. Tall, with a clean-cut appearance, he was half smiling into the morning sun.

I was so amazed to see him that I immediately lowered my window and shouted, "Hey, Roger! It's Judge Lerner-Wren."

Roger turned to me in surprise. His look changed to a giant grin, and he pointed to the knapsack on his back. "Look, Judge, I'm in school," he said and then gave me a wave.

I waved back and wished him well. As I continued my drive to the courthouse, I shook my head in disbelief. And then, I cried.

ACKNOWLEDGMENTS

I want to thank the thousands of men, women, and their family members who have participated in the Broward County Mental Health Court and shared their personal stories of trauma and loss—and recovery. I am humbled by their courage and spirit of resilience, which rises to new heights when the vision of recovery and dignity is established through the court process. I am extremely grateful to Broward County public defender Howard Finkelstein. He listened with his heart to Jane Wynn, as she described her son Aaron's descent into mental illness and incarceration. Howard's realization that our community was ill-equipped to provide care compelled him to spearhead a response. This book reflects the capacity of communities to lead change.

I am most grateful to the leadership of Howard and others, who led the assembly of a local task force seeking criminal justice solutions to those arrested who suffer from serious mental illnesses. This diverse coalition of high-powered and influential stakeholders was resolute in its mission to eliminate silos and integrate two independent and parallel systems of care and, most importantly, to find solutions for the mentally ill. After years of meeting, in spite of many frustrations, new and energized relationships formed to support the establishment of the nation's first mental health court, in Broward County, Florida. I want to acknowledge all those who participated in this process.

I am extremely grateful to the academic scholars in the fields of therapeutic jurisprudence, disability rights, and forensic psychology who supported the court. Their contributions in research and scholarship from a perspective informed by human rights and the experience of trauma were profound, as the court was based on dignity and principles of procedural justice. The transformation of mental health care in America is the centerpiece of the work of the President George W. Bush's New Freedom Commission on Mental Health. I am confident that the vision and promise of excellence in mental health care will be achieved. I wish to express my deep gratitude for the opportunity to serve on the commission.

I am extremely grateful to Joanna Green, my extraordinary editor, for her insights and humanistic vision for this book. I am most appreciative of her guidance and for the privilege of working with Beacon Press. I am also deeply thankful to my agents, Phyllis Parsons and Dana Newman, for their unconditional support of this project.

To my children, Erin and Matthew: you are my muses for the cause of justice and the touchstone of my life's purpose. Finally, to my husband, Dr. Bent Nielsen, who traversed a world for me: your love and support are everything.

NOTES

Author's Note

1. Administrative Order No. VI-97-I-1A, "In re Creation of a Mental Health Court Subdivision within the County Criminal Division, 17th Cir. Ct., Broward., Fla."

2. American Psychiatric Association, *Diagnostic and Statistical Manual of Mental Disorders: IV-TR* (Washington, DC: American Psychiatric Association, 2000).

3. Carol Marbin Miller, "The Woman Who Changed How Disabled People Are Treated Has Died," *Miami Herald*, June 5, 2016.

Chapter 1: A Race for Justice

1. Chapter 394 of the Florida Statutes governs mental health services, including involuntary examination (Section 394.463) and involuntary placement (Section 394.467). The Florida Mental Health Act of 1971, commonly known as the Baker Act (after Representative Maxine Baker, who sponsored the legislation in 1997), allows for involuntary examination of an individual if there is evidence that the person has a mental illness or is a harm to self or others as defined in the statute and is unable or unwilling to provide express informed consent for examination. (Florida Statutes, Section 394.467, as amended in 2016, added a "substantial harm" standard.)

2. National Institute of Drug Courts, "Development and Implementation of Drug Court Systems," Monograph Series 2 (Washington, DC: US Department of Justice, Office of Justice Programs, Drug Courts Program Office, 1999), www.ndci.org/sites/default/files/ndci/Mono2.Systems.pdf.

3. Bruce Winick, "An Agent of Change," videos, parts 1, 2, and 3, YouTube, posted by Cuttingedgelaw.com, September 10, 2009, www.youtube.com/watch?v=EUmdh1uHFg4 (part 1), www.youtube.com/watch?v=-osg8X2KPMY (part 2), https://www.youtube.com/watch?v=ZwZ0xdgF4Ng (part 3).

4. Ibid., part 3.

5. Ibid.

6. Suzanne M. Strong, Ramona Rantala, and Tracey Kyckelhahn, *Census of Problem-Solving Courts*, 2012, bulletin (Washington, DC: US Department of Justice, Office of Justice Programs, Bureau of Justice Statistics, 2016), www.bjs.gov/content/pub/pdf/cpsc12.pdf.

7. Florida Statutes, Section 916.12, states: "A defendant is incompetent to proceed within the meaning of this chapter if the defendant does not have sufficient present ability to consult with her or his lawyer with a reasonable degree of rational understanding or if the defendant has no rational, as well as factual, understanding of the proceedings against her or him."

8. "A New Justice System for the Mentally Ill," *Frontline* website, with link to "The New Asylums," broadcast May 10, 2005, www.pbs.org/wgbh/pages /frontline/shows/asylums/special/courts.html.

9. Florida Grand Jury, *Mental Health Investigation*, interim report, Spring Term, November 9, 1994; Trevor Jensen, "Mental Health System Deplorable, Report Says; Grand Jury Suggests Closing Unit at State Hospital," *Sun-Sentinel*, November 10, 1994.

10. Florida Grand Jury, *Mental Health Investigation*, 9.

11. Ibid., 137–40.

12. Bureau of Justice Statistics, *Medical Problems of Inmates*, 1997, NCJ 181644, January 2001, https://www.bjs.gov/content/pub/ascii/mpi97.txt.

13. Fox Butterfield, "Asylums Behind Bars: A Special Report; Prisons Replace Hospitals for the Nation's Mentally Ill," *New York Times*, March 5, 1998.

14. Ibid.

15. American Psychological Association, *Action for Mental Health: Final Report of the Joint Commission on Mental Illness and Health* (Boston: APA, 1961).

16. John F. Kennedy, "Special Message to Congress on Mental Illness and Mental Retardation, February 5, 1963," American Presidency Project, www .presidency.ucsb.edu/ws/?pid=9546.

17. Risdon N. Slate, Jacqueline K. Buffington-Vollum, and W. Wesley Johnson, *The Criminalization of Mental Illness: Crisis and Opportunity for the Justice System*, 2nd ed. (Durham, NC: Carolina Academic Press, 2013), 38–41.

18. Butterfield, "Asylum Behind Bars."

19. Ibid.

20. "Mental Health a System Priority," *Sun-Sentinel*, June 11, 1993.

21. Sandra Jacobs, "Hospital Prepares for Battle in Crisis over Mental Health, *Sun-Sentinel*, April 30, 1991.

22. Maya Goldman, "Punishment for Prison Misconduct Is Sometimes Death" (New York: Human Rights Watch, May 4, 2017), www.hrw.org/news/2017 /05/04/punishment-prison-misconduct-sometimes-death. See also Human Rights Watch, "Ill-Equipped: US Prisons and Offenders with Mental Illness" (New York: Human Rights Watch, 2003), www.hrw.org/sites/default/files /reports/usa1003.pdf.

Chapter 2: The Shackles Come Off

1. This legal directive was in recognition (1) that mental health resources in Broward County are scarce, (2) that the community-based system of care is highly fragmented, (3) that there is an overrepresentation of people with mental illness in the Broward jail, and (4) that untreated mental illness often leads to incarceration (see Mental Health Court Administrative Order VI-97-1-1A).

2. William A. Anthony, "Recovery from Mental Illness: The Guiding Vision of the Mental Health System in the 1990's," *Psychological Rehabilitation Journal* 16, no. 4 (1993): 11–23.

3. Vincent J. Felitti et al., "Relationship of Childhood Abuse and Household Dysfunction to Many of the Leading Causes of Death in Adults: The Adverse Childhood Experience (ACE) Study," *American Journal of Preventive Medicine* 14, no. 4 (May 1998): 245–58, www.cdc.gov/violenceprevention /acestudy/about_ace.html.

4. Ibid.

5. Centers for Disease Control and Prevention, "Violence Prevention," "About the CDC-Keiser ACE Study," www.cdc.gov/violenceprevention/acestudy /about.html.

6. Ibid.

7. Ibid.

8. Centers for Disease Control and Prevention, "Child Abuse and Neglect: Consequences," www.cdc.gov/violenceprevention/childmaltreatment /consequences.html.

9. Karen Dolan with Jodi L. Carr, "The Poor Get Prison: The Alarming Spread of the Criminalization of Poverty," Institute for Policy Studies, May 18, 2015, www.ips-dc.org/the-poor-get-prison-the-alarming-spread-of-the -criminalization-of-poverty.

10. April Trotter and Margaret Noonan, "Medical Conditions, Mental Health Problems, Disabilities and Mortality Among Jail Inmates," American Jail Association, May 3, 2016, www.usf.edu/cbcs/mhlp/tac/documents/cj-jj/cj /mental-health-problems-among-jail-inmates.pdf.

11. Ibid.

12. Julie Ajinkya, "The Top 5 Facts About Women in Our Criminal Justice System," AmericanProgress.org, March 7, 2012, www.americanprogress.org /issues/women/news/2012/03/07/11219/the-top-5-facts-about-women-in -our-criminal-justice-system/. See also National Resource Center on Justice Involved Women, "Fact Sheet on Justice Involved Women in 2016: Victimization and Experiences of Trauma." "A number of studies have found that about half (50%) of justice involved women report experiencing some kind of physical or sexual abuse in their lifetime, with some studies noted rates of trauma histories as high as 98%."

13. Steven Gold, "Time Trauma and Transformation," TEDxNSU, uploaded April 8, 2016, https://www.youtube.com/watch?v=X7jn1e8Nhzw.

14. David B. Wexler, "Therapeutic Jurisprudence: An Overview," *Thomas M. Cooley Law Review* 17 (2000): 125.

15. See Florida Rules of Criminal Procedure, "Rule 3.213. Continuing Incompetency to Proceed, Except Incompetency to Proceed with Sentencing: Disposition," 2017, http://floridarules.net/florida-rules-of-criminal-procedure/rule-3-213-continuing-incompetency-to-proceed-except-incompetency-to-proceed-with-sentencing-disposition/.

16. Florida Statutes, Section 916.12, (1) "Mental Competency to Proceed," 2016.

17. Michael Braga, Anthony Cormier, and Leonora Lapeter Anton, "Definition of Insanity: Florida Spends Millions Making Sure the Mentally Ill Go to Court—and Gets Nothing for It," *Tampa Bay Times–Herald Tribune*, December 18, 2015.

18. Ibid.

19. Human Rights Watch, "Callous and Cruel: Use of Force Against Inmates with Mental Disabilities in US Jails and Prisons" (New York: Human Rights Watch, May 12, 2015).

20. Florida Rules, "Rule 3.213 (a) Dismissal without Prejudice during Continuing Incompetency," http://floridarules.net/florida-rules-of-criminal-procedure/rule-3-213-continuing-incompetency-to-proceed-except-incompetency-to-proceed-with-sentencing-disposition/.

21. National Suicide Prevention Lifeline, https://suicidepreventionlifeline.org.

22. Florida Policy Institute, "Florida's Provision of Mental Health Services Ranks 49th out of 50 States," February 16, 2016, www.fpi.institute/floridas-provision-of-mental-health-services-ranks-49th-out-of-50-states.

23. Ibid.

24. National Alliance on Mental Illness, "Mental Health by the Numbers," 2013, www.nami.org/Learn-More/Mental-Health-By-the-Numbers.

25. T. R. Insel, "Assessing the Economic Costs of Serious Mental Illness," *American Journal of Psychiatry* 165, no. 6 (2008): 663–65.

26. US Department of Health and Human Services, *Mental Health: A Report of the Surgeon General* (Rockville, MD: US Department of Health and Human Services, Substance Abuse and Mental Health Services Administration, Center for Mental Health Services, National Institute of Mental Health, 1999), https://profiles.nlm.nih.gov/ps/access/NNBBHS.pdf.

Chapter 3: Punishing Loss

1. American College of Obstetricians and Gynecologists, Committee on Health Care for Underserved Women, "Healthcare for Homeless Women," *Women Health Care Physicians*, no. 576, October 2013.

2. J. L. Jasinski et al., *The Experience of Violence in the Lives of Homeless Women: A Research Report* (Orlando: University of Central Florida, 2005).

3. Joan Zorza, "Woman Battering: A Major Cause of Homelessness," *Clearinghouse Review* 25 (1991): 421–27.

4. National Center on Family Homelessness, "The Characteristics and Needs of Families Experiencing Homelessness," (Newton Center, MA: NCFH, 2008), http://files.eric.ed.gov/fulltext/ED535499.pdf.

5. T. P. Baggett et al., "The Unmet Health Care Needs of Homeless Adults: A National Study," *American Journal of Public Health* 100, no. 7 (July 2010): 1326–33.

6. National Coalition for the Homeless, "Substance Abuse and Homelessness: Fact Sheet," www.nationalhomeless.org/factsheets/addiction.pdf.

7. Substance Abuse and Mental Health Services Administration, "Current Statistics on the Prevalence and Characteristics of People Experiencing Homelessness in the United States," July 2011, www.samhsa.gov/sites/default /files/programs_campaigns/homelessness_programs_resources/hrc-factsheet -current-statistics-prevalence-characteristics-homelessness.pdf.

8. On the use of the now-preferred term "justice-involved individual" instead of "criminal," see Jazz Shaw, "White House Wants Colleges to Refer to Criminals as "Justice-Involved Individuals," Hot Air, May 15, 2016, http:// hotair.com/archives/2016/05/15/white-house-wants-colleges-to-refer-to -criminals-as-justice-involved-individuals/; Stephanie S. Covington and Barbara E. Bloom, *Gendered Justice: Women in the Criminal Justice System* (Durham, NC: Carolina Academic Press, 2003).

9. Ibid. See also National Resource on Justice Involved Women, "Fact Sheet on Justice Involved Women 2016," http://cjinvolvedwomen.org/wp-content /uploads/2016/06/Fact-Sheet.pdf.

10. Becki Ney, Rachelle Ramirez, and Marilyn Van Dieten, eds., "Ten Truths That Matter When Working with Justice Involved Women," National Resource Center on Justice Involved Women, April, 2012.

11. National Alliance on Mental Illness, "Jailing People with Mental Illness," www.nami.org/Learn-More/Public-Policy/Jailing-People-with-Mental-Illness.

12. See National Resource Center on Justice Involved Women, "Fact Sheet on Justice Involved Women in 2016," http://cjinvolvedwomen.org/wp-content /uploads/2016/06/Fact-Sheet.pdf.

13. Christine M. Sarteschi, "Mentally Ill Involved with the US Criminal Justice System: A Synthesis," *Sage Open* (online journal), July 16, 2013, http:// journals.sagepub.com/doi/pdf/10.1177/2158244013497029, writes, "A recent study by Greenberg and Rosenheck (2008) notes the prevalence of homelessness among people with SMI is very high (15.3%) and per the authors, was 7.5 to 11.3 times higher than general population."

14. Henry Fitzgerald Jr., "Court a Safety Net for Mentally Ill," *Sun-Sentinel*, December 28, 1998.

15. Lenore E. Walker was the first forensic psychologist to introduce the concept of battered woman syndrome through expert forensic testimony, in the case of Ibn-Tamas v. United States, 407 A.2d 626 (D.C. 1979). On appeal from the trial court's exclusion of her testimony, the DC Court of Appeals

held that the trial court had erred and found that "Dr. Walker's methodology leading to her theory of the Battered Woman Syndrome is generally accepted in the scientific community." Shannon L. Lynch. Dana D. DeHart, Joanne Belknap, and Bonnie L. Green, *Women's Pathways to Jail: The Roles & Intersections of Serious Mental Illness & Trauma*, September 2012, www.bja.gov /publications/womenspathwaystojail.pdf.

16. Sue Reisenger, "Legal Healing," *Miami Herald*, March 26, 2000.

17. Ibid.

18. Ibid.

Chapter 4: *The Raging Voice of Dignity*

1. Michael L. Perlin, "Sanism and the Law," *American Medical Association Journal of Ethics* 15 (October 2013).

2. Ginger Lerner-Wren, "Essays from the Bench—Problem-Solving Justice, Leading Cultural Change and the Restoration of Community," unpublished manuscript, August 2011, in author's collection (based on an interview with Broward County public defender Howard Finkelstein).

3. Ibid.

4. Penny Colman, *Breaking the Chains: The Crusade of Dorothea Lynde Dix* (New York: ASJA Press, 1992).

5. Ibid.

6. Ibid.

7. Dwight D. Eisenhower, "Special Message to the Congress Recommending a Health Program, January 6, 1956," American Presidency Project, www .presidency.ucsb.edu/ws/index.php?pid=10605&st=&st1=.

8. Ibid.

9. Slate, Buffington-Vollum, and Johnson, *Criminalization of Mental Illness*, 38–42.

10. Ibid., 56–57. US Department of Health and Human Services, "Mental Health Myths and Facts,": www.mentalhealth.gov/basics/myths-facts.

Chapter 5: *Simple Dreams*

1. *Sanbourne v. Chiles,* No.89–6283-CIV-NESBITT.

2. Albert Q. Maisel, "Bedlam 1946: Most of US Mental Hospitals Are a Shame and Disgrace," *Life*, May 6, 1946, was an exposé based on two psychiatric state hospitals in Pennsylvania and Ohio. Maisel wrote, "Thousands spend their days—often for weeks at a stretch—locked in devices euphemistically called 'restraints': thick leather handcuffs, great canvas camisoles, 'muffs,' 'mitts,' wristlets, locks and straps and restraining sheets. Hundreds are confined in 'lodges'—bare, bed-less rooms reeking with filth and feces— by day lit only through half-inch holes in steel-plated windows, by night merely black tombs in which the cries of the insane echo unheard from the peeling plaster of the walls."

3. Gonzalez v. Martinez, 756 F. Supp. 1533 (S.D. Fla. 1991), Order on Defendant's Motion for Summary Judgment, executed January 18, 1991, https://scholar.google.com/scholar_case?case=12352836658806527560&hl=en&as_sdt=6&as_vis=1&oi=scholarr.

4. Ibid., 2.

5. Ibid.

6. "Hospital Examiners Broke Down and Cried," *Palm Beach Post*, October 6, 1988.

7. *Gonzalez v. Martinez*, Order on Defendant's Motion for Summary Judgment.

8. Linda Kleindienst, "Mental Hospital to Close; Shutdown in 3 Years Gets Legislative OK," *Sun-Sentinel*, May 28, 1993.

9. Public Law 88–164, "Mental Retardation Facilities and Community Mental Health Centers Construction Act of 1963."

10. John F. Kennedy, "Special Message to Congress on Mental Illness and Mental Retardation, February 5, 1963," American Presidency Project, www.presidency.ucsb.edu/ws/?pid=9546.

11. Ibid.

12. Ibid.

13. The Joint Commission on Mental Health was established in 1955 by the American Psychiatric Association and the American Medical Association. According to Howard R. Goldman and Gerald N. Grob, "Defining Mental Illness in Mental Health Policy," *Health Affairs* 25, no. 3 (May 2006): 737–49, the commission "had a broad mandate" and ultimately focused its study on "medical, psychological, social cultural and other factors related to the cause of mental illness." Per Goldman and Grob, the joint commission ultimately shifted its focus to include a more broad-based focus on the impact of mental health conditions. The final report, published in 1961, *Action for Mental Health*, advanced community-based mental health and laid the groundwork for President Kennedy's national agenda for the Community Mental Health Act of 1963, which emphasized prevention and understanding mental health from a public health perspective. See American Psychological Association, *Action for Mental Health*.

14. Slate, Buffington-Vollum, and Johnson, *Criminalization of Mental Illness*, 37.

15. Ibid.

16. Ibid., 42.

17. Ibid.

18. Michael Winerip, "Bedlam on the Streets," *New York Times*, May 23, 1999.

19. "Kuhn's Big K Stores Plans Wal-Mart Ties," *New York Times*, June 23, 1981.

20. Erin Martz and Will Newbill, "The Rehabilitation of a Hospital: The Transformation of a State Hospital," *International Journal of Psychosocial Rehabilitation* 18, no. 2 (2014), www.psychosocial.com/IJPR_18/Rehab_of_a_hospital_Martz.html.

21. John S. Goldkamp and Cheryl Irons-Guynn, *Emerging Judicial Strategies for the Mentally Ill in the Criminal Caseload: Mental Health Courts in Fort Lauder-*

dale, Seattle, San Bernardino, and Anchorage, report prepared for the US Department of Justice, Office of Justice Programs, Bureau of Justice Assistance (Washington, DC: Department of Justice, April 2000), www.ncjrs.gov /pdffiles1/bja/182504.pdf.

22. Ronald D. Smothers, "Miami Tries Treatment, Not Jail in Drug Cases," *New York Times*, February 19, 1993.

23. "US Department of Justice, Keynote Remarks of the Honorable Janet Reno, Attorney General, Working Luncheon for Consensus Meeting on Drug Treatment in the Criminal Justice System," Omni Shoreham Hotel, Washington, DC, March 24, 1998, www.justice.gov/archive/ag/speeches/1998/0324_agond.htm.

24. Ibid.

25. Henry Fitzgerald Jr.," $18 Million Awarded in Abuse Case," *Sun-Sentinel*, April 4, 1998, articles.sun-sentinel.com/1998–04–04/news/9804040030 _1_medical-care-mental-health-system-verdict.

Chapter 6: I Once Was Lost

1. Broward County Human Services Department, "Comprehensive Community Needs Assessment (Executive Summary)," Public Works LLC, US Census Bureau, American Community Survey, 2012 Data Release, December 2013, http://broward.org/Budget/Documents/NeedsAssesExecSummary June162014.pdf.

2. Numbers based on "Broward by the Numbers," Broward.org, 2015; Jie Zong and Jeanne Batalova, "Caribbean Immigrants in the United States," Metropolitan Policy Institute, September 14, 2016, www.migrationpolicy .org/article/caribbean-immigrants-united-states; National Institute of Mental Health, "Substance Use and Mental Health," www.nimh.nih.gov/health /topics/substance-use-and-mental-health/index.shtml.

3. 1 Ibid.

4. Jeff Jacoby, "The Prison Door Keeps Revolving" *Boston Globe*, May 4, 2014.

5. Mental Health America, "2016 State of Mental Health in Americas— Report Overview Historical Data," www.mentalhealthamerica.net/issues /2016-state-mental-health-america-report-overview-historical-data.

6. Substance Abuse Mental Health Services Agency, "Resilience Annotated Bibliography: SAMHSA's Partners for Recovery Initiative," March 2013, www.samhsa.gov/partners-for-recovery.

7. Danielle Nelson, "Spirituality and Mental Health," *Jamaica Observer*, January 5, 2016, www.jamaicaobserver.com/columns/Spirituality-and-mental -health_47731.

Chapter 7: Therapeutic Justice Goes Mainstream

1. Bruce J. Winick and David B. Wexler, Australian Institute of Judicial Administration, "The Concept of Therapeutic Jurisprudence," http://aija.org .au/index.php/research/australasian-therapeutic-jurisprudence-clearing house/the-concept-of-therapeutic-jurisprudence.

2. Mike Clary, "South Florida's Opioid Overdose Crisis: At Least 800 Expected to Die by End of 2016," *Sun-Sentinel*, November 20, 2016.

3. Corky Siemaszko, "Florida Gov. Declares State's Opioid Epidemic Public Health Emergency," *NBC News*, May 4, 2017.

4. Lawrence Mower, "Failure to Land $10 Million Grant Grates on Sober Home Community," *Palm Beach Post*, December 21, 2016.

5. Vincent J. Felitti et al., "Relationship of Childhood Abuse and Household Dysfunction to Many of the Leading Causes of Death in Adults: The Adverse Childhood Experience (ACE) Study," *American Journal of Preventive Medicine* 14, no. 4 (May 1998): 245–58, www.cdc.gov/violenceprevention /acestudy/about_ace.html.

6. A. Kathryn Power, "Breaking the Silence," *National Council Magazine* 2 (2011), www.thenationalcouncil.org/wp-content/uploads/2012/11/NC-Mag -Trauma-Web-Email.pdf.

7. Ibid.

8. Substance Abuse and Mental Health Services Administration, "SAMHSA's Working Definition of Trauma and Guidance for Principles of a Trauma-Informed Approach," draft report (Rockville, MD: Substance Abuse and Mental Health Services Administration, 2012).

9. J. B. Gillece, "Understanding the Effects of Trauma on Lives of Offenders," *Corrections Today* (June 6, 2012), cited in Chan Noether, "Toward Creating a Trauma-Informed Criminal Justice System," Policy Research Associates, June 6, 2012, www.prainc.com/creating-a-trauma-informed-criminal -justice-system/.

10. H. J. Steadman, "Lifetime Experience of Trauma Among Participants in the Cross-Site Evaluation of the TCE for Jail Diversion Programs Initiative" (unpublished raw data), cited in Noether, "Toward Creating a Trauma-Informed Criminal Justice System."

11. Substance Abuse and Mental Health Services Administration, *Trauma-Informed Care in Behavioral Health Services*, report (SMA) 14-4816, Treatment Improvement Protocols (Rockville, MD: Center for Substance Abuse Treatment, 2014), www.ncbi.nlm.nih.gov/pubmed/24901203.

12. Ibid.

Chapter 8: Brothers and Sisters

1. Lisa Weber-Raley, *On Pins and Needles: Caregiving Adults with Mental Illness*, report prepared by Greenwald & Associates for the National Alliance on Caregiving, Mental Health America, and National Alliance on Mental Illness, February 2016, www.caregiving.org/wp-content/uploads/2016/02 /NAC_Mental_Illness_Study_2016_FINAL_WEB.pdf.

2. The Sibling Leadership Network's mission is "to provide siblings of individuals with disabilities the information, support, and tools to advocate with their brothers and sisters and to promote the issues important to them and their entire families" (see http://siblingleadership.org/).

3. Jennifer Van Pelt, "Aging Parents of Adults with Serious Mental Illness," *Social Work Today* 11, no. 6 (November–December 2011): 18, www.social worktoday.com/archive/111511p18.shtml.

4. Ibid.

5. C. K. Arnold, T. Heller, and J. Kramer, "Support Needs of Siblings of People with Developmental Disabilities, *Intellectual and Developmental Disabilities* 50, no. 5 (2012): 373–82 (see "Siblings of Individuals with Disabilities Fact Sheet").

6. Eun Ha Namking et al., "Well-Being of Sibling Caregivers: Effects of Kinship Relationship and Race," *Gerontologist* (2016): 1–11.

7. Weber-Raley, *On Pins and Needles*.

8. Ibid.

Chapter 9: Changing Hearts and Minds

1. Gayle Bluebird, "History of the Consumer/Survivor Movement," September 11, 1995, www.power2u.org/downloads/HistoryOfTheConsumerMovement .pdf; Clifford Whittingham Beers, *A Mind That Found Itself: An Autobiography* (New York: Longmans, Green, 1908).

2. Lawrence Van Gelder, "Howard Geld, 42, Advocate for Mentally Ill, Dies," *New York Times*, February 14, 1995.

3. Pamela G. Hardin et al., "White Paper: US Peer Leadership & Workforce Development," *NACBHDD Newsletter*, June 2014, https://jenpadron .com/2014/06/03/white-paper-us-peer-leadership-and-workforce -development/.

4. Patrick Hendry, Common Threads, *Stories of Survival & Recovery from Mental Illness*, Florida Peer Network and Louis de la Parte Florida Mental Health Institute, 2007, www.floridatac.com/files/document/Common%20Threads %2012.18.07%20Final.pdf.

5. See Peer Support Coalition of Florida, www.peersupportfl.org/.

6. See Florida Certification Board, "Certified Recovery Peer Specialist," flcerti-ficationboard.org/wp-content/uploads/CRPS-Candidate-Guide-2015.pdf.

7. Ibid.

8. Eric R. Maisel, "Jennifer Maria Padron on Peer Support and Peer Services: On the Future of Mental Health," *Psychology Today*, April 27, 2016, www .psychologytoday.com/blog/rethinking-mental-health/201604/jennifer -maria-padron-peer-support-and-peer-services.

Chapter 10: A Rush to Privatization

1. Michael Mayo, "Rushed Privatization Plan Will Harm Broward's Mentally Ill," column, *Sun-Sentinel*, August 8, 2011.

2. Brittany Davis, "State in a Rush to Hand Over Mental Health Contracts to Private Sector," *Florida Health News*, August 19, 2011, http://health.wusf .usf.edu/post/state-rush-hand-over-mental-health-contracts-private-sector #stream/0.

3. Ibid.

4. Ibid.

5. Robert Paulson et al., "Evaluation of the Florida DCF Community-Based Care Initiative," University of South Florida, Mental Health Law and Faculty Publications, June 16, 2003, www.dcf.state.fl.us/admin/publications /docs/cbc_report_091503.pdf.

6. Florida Tax Watch, "Analysis of Florida's Behavioral Health Managing Entity Model," March 2015, http://floridataxwatch.org/resources/pdf/Managing EntitiesFINAL.pdf.

7. Florida Statutes, Section 394.9082, "Behavioral Health Managing Entities," www.leg.state.fl.us/Statutes/index.cfm?App_mode=Display_Statute &Search_String=&URL=0300-0399/0394/Sections/0394.9082.html.

8. Charles Palmer et al., "Effective Public Management of Mental Health Care: Views from States on Medicaid Reforms That Enhance Service Integration and Accountability," Milbank Fund and Bazelon Center for Mental Health, May 2000, www.milbank.org/wp-content/uploads/2016/06/Effective -Public-Management-of-Mental-Health-Care.pdf.

9. Ron Honberg et al., *State Mental Health Cuts: A National Crisis*, report prepared for National Alliance on Mental Illness," March 2011, www.nami .org/getattachment/About-NAMI/Publications/Reports/NAMIStateBudget Crisis2011.pdf, 1, 2.

10. Ibid.

11. Lawrence B. Solum, "Procedural Justice," *Southern California Law Review* 78, no. 1 (November 2004): 181–321.

12. Ibid.

13. Mayo, "Rushed Privatization Plan."

14. Ibid.

Chapter 11: In Honor of Our Elders

1. National Coalition for the Homeless, "Homelessness Among Elderly Persons" (Washington, DC: September 2009), www.nationalhomeless.org /factsheets/Elderly.pdf.

2. Adam Nagourney, "Old and on the Street: The Graying of America's Homeless," *New York Times*, May 31, 2016.

3. Ibid.

4. "Point of View: Homeless Elderly Statistics Frightening," *Palm Beach Post*, June 26, 2014.

5. Broward County Housing Authority website, on the page "Broward County Housing Authority Waiting Lists," announces that wait lists for all the housing programs are closed as of February 2017, and there are three thousand names on the list with a lottery for available units. See https://affordable housingonline.com/housing-authority/Florida/Broward-County-Housing -Authority/FL079.

6. Broward.org, "Celebrating Diversity in Broward County," www.broward
.org/CelebratingDiversity/Pages/Default.aspx (citing data from the 2010 US
census).

7. See Daniel E. Jimenez et al., "Cultural Beliefs and Mental Health Treatment
Preferences of Ethnically Diverse Older Adult Consumers in Primary Care,"
American Journal of Geriatric Psychiatry 20, no. 6 (June 2012): 533–42.

8. Temple Collaborative on Community Inclusion, "Cultural Competence in
Mental Health," May 8, 2017, http://tucollaborative.org/sdm_downloads
/cultural-competence-in-mental-health/.

9. Centers for Disease Control, "Understanding Elder Abuse: Fact Sheet,"
www.cdc.gov/violenceprevention/pdf/em-factsheet-a.pdf.

10. Centers for Disease Control, National Center for Injury Prevention and
Control, Division of Violence Prevention, "Understanding Elder Abuse Fact
Sheet, 2016," www.cdc.gov/violenceprevention/pdf/empfactsheet-a.pdf.

11. *Sanbourne v. Chiles*, No.89–6283-CIV-NESBITT.

12. Rob Barry et al., "Neglected to Death, Part 1: Once Pride of Florida; Now
Scenes of Neglect," *Miami Herald*, April 30, 2011.

13. Michael Sallah and Carol Marbin Miller, "Florida Lawmakers Consider
Tough Law to Protect Assisted Living Facilities," *Tampa Bay Times*, January
18, 2012.

Chapter 12: The Power of Human Connection

1. The New Freedom Commission on Mental Health was assembled by President George W. Bush in 2002. The commission's mission was to study the
US mental health service delivery system and recommend improvements
to enable adults with serious mental illness and children with a serious
emotional disturbance to live, work, learn and participate fully in their
communities. For the final report to the president, *Achieving the Promise:
Transforming Mental Health Care in America*, see http://govinfo.library.unt
.edu/mentalhealthcommission/reports/reports.htm.

2. Paula McMahon, "Court Stand on Mental Illness Wins High Marks," *Sun-
Sentinel*, September 8, 2000.

3. Norman G. Poythress et al., "Perceived Coercion and Procedural Justice in
the Broward Mental Health Court," *International Journal of Law and Psychiatry* 25 (2002): 517–33. Researchers noted, "The Broward Court was
designed to be informal, often involving interaction, and dialogue between
the participant about problems and treatment options. . . . The patience and
tolerance . . . create an impression that speedy disposition of a large number
of cases is not a priority."

4. Ibid.

5. Abe Stein, "How Home Plate Lives Up to Its Name," *Atlantic*, March 31, 2014.

6. Judith Hibbard and Helen Gilburt, *Supporting People to Manage Their Health:
An Introduction to Patient Activation*, report prepared for the King's Fund,

May 2014, www.kingsfund.org.uk/sites/default/files/field/field_publication
_file/supporting-people-manage-health-patient-activation-may14.pdf.

7. Ibid., 4.

8. Ibid., 13,14.

9. Ginger Lerner-Wren, "Raising the Bar for Suicide Prevention," Director's Corner, Suicide Prevention Resource Center, October 7, 2016, www.sprc .org/news/mental-health-courts-raising-bar-suicide-prevention. This article describes why mental health courts are in an important position to advance suicide prevention. "Zero Suicide is a commitment to suicide prevention in health and behavioral health care systems and is also a specific set of strategies and tools." See http://zerosuicide.sprc.org/.

10. National Suicide Prevention Hotline, https://suicidepreventionlifeline.org/.

11. Per the National Council for Behavioral Health, "Whole Health Action Management," www.thenationalcouncil.org/training-courses/whole-health -action-management/, "Whole Health Action Management (WHAM) training is a peer-led intervention for people with chronic health and behavioral health conditions that activates self-care management to create and sustain new healthy behaviors."

12. Ibid.

Chapter 13: A Crying Shame

1. Boris Sanchez and Kevin Conlon, "North Miami Shooting: Autistic Man Suffers in Aftermath, Mom Says," CNN, July 27, 2016.

2. Charles Rabin, "How a Broom-Swinging Mentally Ill Man Ended Up Shot Dead by Police," *Miami Herald*, February 16, 2015.

3. See Cynthia Golembeski and Robert Fullilove, "Criminal (In)Justice in the City and Its Associated Health Consequences," *American Journal of Public Health* 95, no. 10 (October 1995): 1701–6, http://ajph.aphapublications .org/doi/pdf/10.2105/AJPH.2005.063768.

4. Peter Wagner and Bernadette Rabuy, "Mass Incarceration: The Whole Pie 2017," Prison Policy Initiative press release, March 14, 2017, www.prison policy.org/reports/pie2017.html.

5. Golembeski and Fullilove, "Criminal (In)Justice in the City and Its Associated Health Consequences."

6. Ibid.

7. Allen S. Noonan, Hector Eduardo Velasco-Mondragon, and Fernando A. Wagner, "Improving the Health of African Americans in the USA: An Overdue Opportunity for Social Justice," *Public Health Reviews* 37 (2016): 12, https://publichealthreviews.biomedcentral.com/articles/10.1186 /s40985–016–0025–4.

8. US Department of Health and Human Services, US Public Health Service, "Executive Summary, Mental Health: Culture, Race, and Ethnicity—A Supplement to Mental Health: A Report of the Surgeon General" (Rockville,

MD: US Department of Health and Human Services, Public Health Service, Office of the Surgeon General, n.d.), www.ct.gov/dmhas/lib/dmhas /publications/mhethnicity.pdf), iv.

9. Ibid., 11.

10. Ibid., 5.

11. On the so-called Baker Act, see chapter 1, note 1.

Chapter 14: A Referendum on Hope

1. Senate Bill 1865—106th Congress: America's Law Enforcement and Mental Health Project, A bill to provide grants to establish demonstration mental health courts," www.govtrack.us/congress/bills/106/s1865; see also https:// www.govtrack.us/congress/bills/106/s1865/summary. The bill was signed into law by President Bill Clinton on November 13, 2000.

2. Ibid.

3. Substance Abuse Mental Health Services Administration, "SAMHSA's Working Definition of Recovery; 10 Guiding Principles of Recovery," August 2010, https://store.samhsa.gov/shin/content/PEP12-RECDEF/PEP12 -RECDEF.pdf.

4. The National Alliance on Mental Illness, "NAMI Warns Senate About Criminalization of Mental Illness, Supports Cornyn Bill," February 10, 2016, www .nami.org/Press-Media/Press-Releases/2016/NAMI-Warns-Senate -about-Criminalization-of-Mental.

5. White House, "Executive Order: New Freedom Commission on Mental Health," April 29, 2002, https://georgewbush-whitehouse.archives.gov /news/releases/2002/04/20020429-2.html. "Sec. 3. Mission. The mission of the Commission shall be to conduct a comprehensive study of the United States mental health service delivery system, including public and private sector providers, and to advise the President on methods of improving the system. The Commission's goal shall be to recommend improvements to enable adults with serious mental illness and children with serious emotional disturbances to live, work and participate fully in their communities."

6. National Institute of Mental Health, "Any Mental Illness (AMI) among US Adults," www.nimh.nih.gov/health/statistics/prevalence/any-mental-illness -ami-among-adults.shtml.

7. Matt Ford, "America's Largest Mental Hospital Is a Jail," *Atlantic*, June 8, 2016. According to the Treatment Advocacy Center, "Serious Mental Illness Prevalence in Jails and Prisons," background paper, September 2016, "Overall approximately 20% of inmates in jail and 15% of inmates in state prisons are estimated to have a serious mental illness." Calculating from the total jail population, this means that approximately 383,000 individuals with serious mental illness are behind bars in the United States.

8. American Psychological Association, "Why Philadelphia's Mental Health Successes Should Spur Capitol Hill to Action," Psychology Benefits Society,

May 1, 2014, https://psychologybenefits.org/2014/05/01/why-philadelphias-mental-health-successes-should-spur-capitol-hill-to-action.

9. New Freedom Commission on Mental Health, *Achieving the Promise: Transforming Mental Health Care in America*, final report to the White House, July 22, 2003, govinfo.library.unt.edu/mentalhealthcommission/reports/FinalReport/downloads/FinalReport.pdf.

10. Ibid.

11. World Health Organization, "mhGAP: Mental Health Gap Action Programme—Scaling Up Care for Mental, Neurological, and Substance Use Disorders," 2002, www.who.int/mental_health/mhgap_final_english.pdf.

12. Victoria de Menil, in "Reforming Kenya's Ailing Mental Health System: In Conversation with Victoria de Menil," Africa Research Institute, June 27, 2013, www.africaresearchinstitute.org/newsite/blog/mental-health-in-kenya, describes how, on May 12, 2013, forty patients escaped from Mathari Hospital in Nairobi. The incident attracted widespread coverage about the conditions in Mathari and the shortcomings of mental health care in the country. Of the annual budget, only 0.5 percent is allocated to mental health provisions. Menil notes that Kenyan mental health advocates are seeking a community-based care approach to promote human rights.

13. Michael L. Perlin, "There Are No Trials Inside the Gates of Eden: Mental Health Courts, the Convention on the Rights of Persons with Disabilities, Dignity, and the Promise of Therapeutic Jurisprudence," in *Coercive Care: Rights, Law, and Policy*, ed. Bernadette McSherry and Ian Freckelton (New York: Routledge, 2015).

14. McSherry and Freckelton, *Coercive Care*, 2.

15. Ibid., 11.

16. Michelle Edgely, "Why Do Mental Health Courts Work? A Confluence of Treatment, Support & Adroit Judicial Supervision," *International Journal of Law and Psychiatry* 37, no. 6 (2014): 572–80.

17. Ibid.

18. Ibid., 4.

19. Florida Grand Jury, "Mental Health Investigation," interim report, Spring Term, November 9, 1994.

Chapter 15: Recovery Is Real

1. Debbie Plotnick is vice president for mental health and systems advocacy at Mental Health America and provides leadership for mental health systems advocacy initiatives within the group's affiliate network.

2. Florida Grand Jury, *Mental Health Investigation*, interim report, Spring Term, November 9, 1994.

3. Fox Butterfield, "Asylums Behind Bars: A Special Report: Prisons Replace Hospitals for the Nation's Mentally Ill," *New York Times*, March 5, 1998.